THE GREAT *Human* REBRAND

How to Step Out of the Labels That Divide Us
and Into the Humanity That Unites Us

Merry Carole Powers

To the duchess, the magician, and the unicorn.

Thank you for this life enchanted.

CONTENTS

Confessions of a Label Maker

It's no easy thing to figure out who you are in a world that's constantly telling you who you should be. I ought to know. For a long time, I've been one of the people doing the telling.

As a creative director and leader in global branding and advertising, it's been my job to convince you that who you are and what you have is not enough. If you turned on the TV, I was there with a commercial. If you were surfing the web, I was there with a banner ad. If you were wandering YouTube, I was there with a video. If you were checking email, I was there with a message. I was always there—in the form of a giant billboard, quick tweet, thoughtful blog, unexpected post, or onslaught of snackable reels and stories, all of which were designed to entice you into believing that there was a better experience or a better you just waiting in the wings of your life. A more youthful you is just an injection away. A more athletic you is just a sneaker away. The more powerful chick magnet in you is just a light beer away.

The creatives who sit at the epicenter of the $500 billion global branding business are master label makers. We know exactly how to take a product and give it a fancy look and a good story. We make it stand for an experience or a way of life that speaks to your hopes and dreams. Then, through that, convince you, by the millions, to join our ranks, pay our prices, and spread our word. As a result, we keep cash registers ringing and C-suites smiling.

Now, to be fair, advertising is not all shallow and profit driven. We help brands do a lot of good as well. Through purpose and mission-driven thinking, creative thinking has raised awareness and driven change for everything from equal pay and feeding the hungry to protecting the environment and democratizing access to education, water and health care. Whether being used for profit or purpose, the point I'm making here is that we have a very sought-after skill, that being the ability to influence minds and manipulate behavior.

When deployed correctly, labels hold the power to sway the masses, which explains why pretty much every major institution on the planet engages in this same practice in one way or another. I can spot a fellow label maker a mile away, and trust me when I tell you, we good people of the branding world are not the only ones tapping into the power of manipulation.

Institutions everywhere are wielding their labels to tell you how to live and what to believe. Religious organizations decide to whom we pray. Political parties mandate how we should vote. The entertainment industry tells us how to look and what to weigh. Educational institutions dictate the manner in which we must learn. The list goes on and on. Just as the world of advertising uses product labels to promote financial agendas, other institutions across our culture use human labels to promote their agendas, be that to grow a belief system, win an election, or popularize an organization.

When I first saw how far-reaching manipulation by labels was, it shocked me. Then, it sort of shamed me. I didn't like being part of the problem. Eventually, however, it actually inspired me, and I recognized that I could be part of the solution instead. If I knew how to help brands construct labels to convince people to behave a certain way, then I also had the power to help people deconstruct those same labels and, in turn, dial up immunity to that kind of manipulation. And that led to this book.

In *The Great Human Rebrand*, I pull back the curtain and give you a look at how labels work behind the scenes. And in doing so, I hope that we, both individually and collectively, begin to take back some of our power. Because the labels we wear are making us weak and susceptible to deep division. Male. Female. Black, White. Liberal. Conservative. Immigrant. Citizen. With every label we wear, we separate ourselves into opposing camps. And with each camp we draw another line in the sand, adopting another lens that distorts our view and justifies our senseless habit of judging one another. This divides us. It weakens us. It opens us up to all manner of profiling and stereotyping that then ripples out through business, health care, and public safety systems, creating unfair practices and an imbalanced world.

These labels we identify with might be a part of who we are, but not one of them can come close to encompassing all a given person is. You would have to shrink yourself very small in order to fit into any one label. There is more to each of us than our current societal perspectives would have us believe. And if we can see more, we can connect more. And connection fosters strength. United, we can begin to collectively find safety, garnish strength, and create the solidarity we need to make lasting change. Opening our eyes to the power labels hold over us is so important, particularly at this juncture in time. Because our labels are now running amok, and the damage this is doing is hitting critical mass.

Labels are no longer words that simply describe us. We've begun to let our labels define us. Definitions and descriptions are not the same thing. A description of something is general and open to interpretation. It can change over time. But a definition is exact, enduring, and meant to tell you precisely what something is all about. No single word should have the power to tell you who you are—only you get to decide that.

Human labels are subsets. They're little slivers of self that, when over identified with, diminish our ability to access the full power and potential of all we are and all the ways we can come together to make lasting change. Collectively, we are powerful. But every time we fragment into a subsection of ourselves, our personal and collective strength becomes fragmented as well.

It's time to cut the puppet strings and toss our labels into a dumpster fire. We're meant to control our own minds. We're meant to create our own thoughts. We're meant to be a team, living this thing called Life together. But we'll never get there with so many labels standing between us. I hope this book helps you see the depth of this fact. And the depth of who you are. Because there's so much more to each of us than the label makers of the world would have us believe. And we, as a human race, deserve more than a world designed to divide us.

PART 1

Labels and Their Lies

Labels, the titles we use to define ourselves as people, races, nations, and everything in between, are tearing our world apart. They may have once served a positive purpose, but that day is gone. Every label we wear is creating disfunction in our world: gender labels have us tiptoeing around one another; race labels have us killing one another; nationality labels have us caging one another at borders; political labels have us storming our own halls of democracy; religious labels have us fighting over a peaceful God; disability labels have us focusing on what someone can't do rather than what they can; sexual orientation labels have us attempting to outlaw love, which in a fantastically ironic twist, happens to be the Universe's principle law.

What was once used to differentiate us into categories is now dividing us into camps—angry, hurt, fed up, confused, worn out, flabbergasted camps. And all those feelings, justified or not, are widening the divide and weakening our connection to the one thing that matters: each other.

This cultural operating system is creating a social infection that is embedded deeper than just the macro labeling of things like race and gender. There are endless micro labels, on every level imaginable, that are driving the way we think about ourselves and each other. Zip codes, a simple series of numbers, can label us as poor or prestigious. Swooshes on shoes define our athleticism. Even something as random as ivy wields power to divide us into leagues of intelligence which for the record, is as arbitrary as it is inaccurate. Just because you have more money to spend on an education doesn't necessarily make you more intelligent. Opportunity can be bought. Intelligence is innate.

I hope you're picking up what I'm laying down. Labels are much more powerful than you might think. It's important to understand the depth of this power because it's a force that's woven into every system and synapse firing on the planet. And as a result, labels are being wielded in order to manipulate your mind and influence your behavior, often without you even realizing it.

A genuine understanding as to how this works means starting at the beginning, when labels weren't actually powerful at all. At their most fundamental level, labels are fairly harmless—simple communicators that allow us to create a basic understanding of something. Without them, we wouldn't know what aisle the baked beans are in at the grocery store, or which file to open when we look at the folders on our computer. When used to categorize, labels enable our brains to organize information and make sense of things. There is no deeper meaning to the label. It's neither good nor bad that there is a grocery store section labeled "produce." It's a neutral piece of information, and we don't feel one way or another about it.

However, labels, as we most often use them, are anything but neutral. Across our culture they have come to represent far more than their original intent. Viewing a person as Black or white doesn't simply refer to the color of their skin. The words "Black" and "white" are no longer just categorical. Long ago they became cultural in nature—each carrying a label that implied judgment and internal bias. And once that happened, a systematic superiority was sown into those labels, which, for centuries, has given those with power and influence the ability to dole out privilege at will.

The practice of manipulating labels to benefit a group is not exclusive to race. Religions and governments play the game as well. In religion, labels such as "the faithful" and "the chosen" are used to generate loyalty and influence behavior. People choose to adopt one of these religious labels and, because they believe they are among a select and elite few, the "chosen," feel a moral superiority over those who practice other religions. This, in turn, has pitted personal belief against personal belief with the grand prize being a one-way ticket to eternal salvation. As a result, mosques, temples, churches, and women's health care facilities have been bombed in the name of religion.

In government, party labels such as Republican and Democrat have become so politically charged that they've mushroomed into sub-labels such as "blue" states and "red" states and right-wingers and left-wingers. The polarization is so extreme that it has many of us openly bullying and attacking one another and acting like both wings don't actually belong to the same bird.

Every set of labels mentioned holds the power to start wars. Every one of them has. And their ability to catalyze people and incite violence doesn't come from the category the label was originally intended to designate. The discord comes from the man-made meanings, both overt and implied, that have been instilled into the labels over time. These deeply-seeded and emotionally charged belief systems the labels have come to represent are the undercurrents of the divisiveness tearing our world apart. They are the strings that the puppeteers of power are using to control world stages.

Somewhere along the line we, as a human race, started buying the hype. We stopped questioning why the world looks at and labels things in certain ways and simply started accepting them. Belief systems became operating systems. Operating systems that, in turn, have been baked into our corporate, educational, economic, political, and structural institutions. And the more that people bought into those meanings, the more justification was given to their existence. Entire ways of life have been built around these mindsets that are, at their core, false and misleading. Labels are loaded with lies. And the deception runs deep.

Let's look at race as an example, because it is one of the most important labels to deconstruct. Rather than just letting the label "black" refer to the color of skin, someone, somewhere, assigned meaning to it. Completely without any sort of data or common sense to back it up, it was decided that Black people were somehow inferior to white people. It's completely ridiculous, but the idea stuck. It caught on and grew stronger.

This led to organized rules governing who should be free versus enslaved, where a person wasn't allowed to sit, eat, learn, or live. It ushered in assumptions about what a person's intentions were when walking down a street and what opportunities they were eligible for. None of this judgment or toxic behavior can be linked to the label itself. The word black is a simple descriptor. Black means black and nothing more. It doesn't mean dangerous or lazy or inferior or any other completely false and random characteristic. Everything else that's come to be associated with it is a man-made creation based on absolutely nothing but opinion. And small-minded opinion at that. It's false information. Fake news. But as is the intention of fake news, it has misled people and as a result, an entire way of being has unfolded that has created immense disparity and heartache over the course of centuries.

Looking beyond race, it's not hard to see that this same pattern can be applied to many things across our entire culture: men versus women, Christians versus Muslims, rich versus poor, gay versus straight, magic versus muggle. We've allowed these labels to pit us against one another. The associations we've infused into our cultural labels feed the disparagement and divisiveness of our world to an incredibly powerful degree.

At some unfortunate juncture in our evolution we have stopped seeing each other as humans and started judging each other as labels. Because of that, labels now create hierarchy instead of order. People have decided that one skin color is better than the other. One name for God is truer than another. One gender is stronger than the other. One expression of love is more acceptable than another. And with these decisions, lines have been drawn in the sand and sides have been taken. Players become invested in being right and look for evidence and justification that their label is the best label. This pattern of thinking has been perpetuated and passed down from generation to generation to the point we, having been born into it, simply accept it as the natural way of things. But there is nothing natural about hate, judgment, superiority, or prejudice—these little gems are strictly man-made.

Most labels governing our world right now—or at least the most influential ones we associate with—have been inherited. Their structures, limitations, and expectations were established before we were even born. Long before learning to think for ourselves, we began to think in the ways the ingrained labels of the world influenced us to think. We stopped questioning why certain ideas were attached to certain people and started operating as if the beliefs were truth. Which means that, from our first breath, labels hijacked our ability to think autonomously and make decisions based on personal experience.

Think about that for a second, because it's important. What I'm telling you is that some of your core beliefs might not even exist if, from the get-go, you were not being swayed by the deceptive outside influences of our culture. I hope that makes you question a few things, because if we are going to come back together as a human race, and if you are going to evolve and develop personally, there are plenty of things that need questioning.

The systematic labeling in our world has kept us from truly seeing one another. Think of it like being inside a clear bubble. Technically, it's transparent and you can see the world around you. But the fact is, there is a filter between you and the world that is imperceptibly skewing your viewpoint. You think you are seeing things clearly, when in truth you are removed from the reality of it, living in your own little bubble.

Now, put a couple billion people together in that bubble and the thinking takes on a life of its own. Subcultures arise and become stronger based on how many people share those ideas, how deeply they're held, and what sort of treatments, positive or negative, these groups have received based on investing in the shared consciousness. If you have been rewarded by the label's lie, then you will fight harder to defend its existence and keep your rewarded ways of working in place. If you have been persecuted for it, you will fight harder to tear down the system that is treating you unfairly or holding you back. Either way, we continue fighting with one another.

Whether our culture's labels are working to your benefit or your detriment, by putting your energy into them, you're contributing to the growing divide that is tearing us apart. Marginalization breeds resentment. Privilege breeds elitism. On both ends of the spectrum the power of belonging to a label results in catalyzing people—driving behavior that is fighting a *way* of life rather than respecting a human life. Because of this dynamic, our stances have become so emotionally charged that they are triggers. And since triggers are designed to be pulled . . . Boom.

Here we are, living in a world of violence, both overt and covert, that's costing us on every front. It's costing us our sanity. Our solidarity. Our humanity. Our environment. And financially, the price we're paying is staggering. The Institute for Economics and Peace estimates violence costs the world $14 trillion every year.[1] How many homeless people might we feed with $14 trillion? How many scholarship funds might be established and how many schools might be able to pay teachers a living wage? And that $14 trillion only covers the physical violence. The mental and emotional violence we subject one another to carry costs all their own—both personally and professionally.

Potential lost value from people problems are upwards of $52.5 million a year[2] for corporations in the United States. Many of these problems stem from discrimination, profiling, harassment, and bias, all of which focus on labels. Diversity, equity, and inclusion initiatives all work to help ensure that we are not being corralled or limited by the labels we wear, all a critical first step in undoing systems of quiet violence that kill opportunity for so many. But it is just a first step. Once we ensure that companies see us as individuals and not labels, we must ensure that they develop us at that level as well.

Policies that ensure diversity in hiring only get people in the door. Once inside, reaching potential means peeling back the labels that make them diverse on the surface and digging deeper to lead from the strengths that live below that surface. Those hires have to learn how much more there is to them than meets the eye. Focusing on the surface labels makes it impossible to mine the depths of human individuality, which is where our true talents and passions live.

The time has come in our human evolution to take things to a new level. And, in case you haven't noticed, the Universe has been about as subtle as a freight train in delivering that message. This reminder is popping up everywhere from #MeToo to Black Lives Matter. The circumstances may differ, but the underlying message of the riots, marches, and movements is the same: Equality over elitism. Kindness over corruption. Decency over denigration. Acceptance over assholisim. In other words, love over labels.

Our time of reckoning is actually a time of recognizing. We are being called to start seeing one another for who we really are—human beings with a depth and commonality that cannot be contained by a set of labels. We are more than our genders, our races, our religions, and our disabilities. We are more than our resumes, our political parties, and our nationalities. We are all human beings. Individuals with hopes and dreams and talents and quirks and families and friends and every right to live in fairness and freedom.

Our idea of love may differ, but the heart that beats with the emotion is the same. Our personal dreams may differ, but the joy we feel at experiencing them is

---

1   World Economic Forum: Conflict Costs the Global Economy $14 Trillion a Year.
2   Harvard Business Review: Putting a Price on People Problems at Work.

the same. The name of our god may differ, but the belief that there is something greater at play in the world is the same. Our language may differ, but the need to express and to feel understood is the same. Our skin color may differ, but the human spirit alive beneath it is the same.

When the COVID-19 pandemic hit in 2019, labels didn't hold sway. The virus didn't find the rich more worthy of health than the poor. It could not have cared less which flag a person saluted, where anyone fell on the gender spectrum, or who was or wasn't disabled. It held no respect for national or international borders. The virus leveled the playing field of life. And in doing so, for a brief moment in time, it put us all on the same page.

We all heard over and over again, "We are in this together," which for so many of us was genuinely believed. We sang from our balconies and hung words of inspiration on our windows. We flashed our lights on and off and banged our pans in universal appreciation for the essential workers who found themselves unexpectedly on the front lines. In spite of all the madness, incredible acts of humanity took place worldwide.

This is the magic of unity. When we stop focusing on the things that divide us, we can connect on a more human level. And with that, a sense of solidarity takes root. Team spirit kicks in. We start having each other's back instead of putting a knife in each other's back. It's a shift of our shared mindset and an evolution of the heart, and it's the direction Life is pointing us in.

The fact of the matter is, we are deeply connected to one another. We breathe the same air, walk the same earth, and rely on the same rhythmic heartbeat to keep us alive. This is a simple human truth. Currently, our world doesn't value the truth. It still clings to the dishonesty it has long lived by. And we can thank labels for so many of these lies.

CHAPTER 1

The Three Little Fibs

Labels are liars. The ways in which they misrepresent truth are many, but if you chase the source back far enough, it usually leads to one of three fundamental fibs. The first of which is what you see is what you get.

The core deception here is the assumption that people are little more than meets the eye. Believing this opens the door for you to make snap judgments based on immediate, superficial glimpses. For example, if someone drives a fancy car, the first little fib would lead you to the quick conclusion that that person is successful and wealthy. It could just as easily be that rather than a mountain of money, that person has a mountain of debt from driving around in a car they can't afford. Or maybe it's a rental, or borrowed, or stolen. The truth is, we have no clue about who the person behind the wheel is, but our minds automatically assume based on what we have come to believe about the label of the car.

Labels are liars and, therefore, can't be trusted. We've all had experiences that prove this to be true. Have you ever bought a bottle of wine because you liked the label only to be totally disappointed by what's inside? I have. Pretty much every time I get sucked in like that, I end up pouring the wine, and the money that bought it, right down the drain. Similar in experience, I've taken jobs at top-name shops that turned out to be third-rate experiences and dated men who looked pretty on the surface but were nothing but ugly on the inside. Each time, I was tricked by the "what you see is what you get" con. Conversely, some of the no-name clothes in my wardrobe are better than many of my designer-brand pieces, and a few of the most scatterbrained people I've ever met have pedigreed diplomas hanging on their walls. By focusing on the surface of things, labels mislead us into assuming we can know someone or something simply by looking at it. And, in this instance, in addition to being liars, labels are thieves because they rob us of the deeper connections that could be available to us.

Very little of life's richness can be found on its surface. If you never looked past the surface of the ocean, for example, you'd only see water and miss the incredible technicolor world of coral reefs, kelp forests, and trillions of amazing creatures living there. The most spectacular part can only be discovered by diving deeper.

We are all oceans unto ourselves. We, too, have vast worlds and untold riches teeming beneath our surface. But we live in a label-loving world that perpetuates surface living, so we barely break through. Human connection and development cannot happen on the surface of life. Just like gold, you have to dig to unearth your treasure. If you think your looks, your wardrobe, the number of social media followers you have, the color of your skin, the country you were born in, or the job title on your business card tells the story of all you are, then not only are labels lying to you but you are lying to yourself.

Your obvious descriptors shed little to no real light on who you really are. Beneath the surface of your labels are the things that truly define you. Your innate talents. Your personal values. Your deep and abiding passions. Your hidden wounds. Even your peculiar, oddball quirks. These are the truth of who you are. And no one is ever going to get to know them simply by just looking at you.

Values, talents, passions, quirks, fears, dreams, unexplainable interests—all are rooted in your essence. As such, expressing them is *essential*—absolutely necessary for anyone to truly be themselves. These are what make you unlike anyone else. Ironically, they're also what connect you to everyone. A personal essence is something every single one of us possesses. When we start to recognize this, we can relate to others. When we relate, we can connect. When we connect, we can collaborate. When we collaborate, we can change everything.

But all too often our ability to connect and collaborate is thwarted because true connection requires a certain amount of depth. And as a race, we have become comfortable living on the surface of life. Surface living is quick. Easy. Requires less effort. Connecting only with the outward aspects in one another is the fast-food version of coexisting. It gets the job done but in the long run, it also creates an unhealthy world. Healthy connection requires a deeper dive into the real ingredients of who a person is. Generally, this means first diving deeper into yourself. And this can be uncomfortable.

There are often hard things waiting for you when you dig beneath the surface of who you are. Usually, the first among them is your own baloney. The personal regrets, the worn out resentments, and the self-deprecating stories you have been telling yourself will all be there to greet you when you start to get real about who you are. And there are two things I have to say about that: One, don't sweat it— we're all baloney factories. Every person on this earth carries around unhealthy, emotional byproducts from being alive. And two, it's totally worth slogging through your own braunschweiger. Because on the other side, you are going to find tremendous strengths.

Pushing past your weaknesses to claim your strengths epitomizes personal and professional development. As coming pages will show, bringing your true self to the surface is the best way to debunk the first lie labels tell.

THE SECOND FIB

In addition to being innately superficial, labels are fluent in stereotyping. Which brings us to the second lie labels tell. Unlike some lies, which are specific, stereotypes are ambiguous. They use generality to deceive. These lies take vast groups of humans, lump them together into a singular unit, and then tell you that they are all the same: jocks are stupid; Muslims are terrorists; women are emotional; gay men are bitchy; Black men are dangerous; blondes have more fun. The list of falsehoods goes on and on.

You would not have to look very far into any one of those stereotypes to find an exception to its rule. And then another one. And another one. And on it would go until you'd have no choice but to admit the label is a puddle of nonsense.

Obviously, sweeping generalizations that assign individual characteristics to entire groups of people can't ever be accurate, but for some reason, we as a culture tend to buy into them anyway. And when we do, we set ourselves up for failure, because again, the little lie isn't as harmless as it seems. What stereotypes lack in accuracy they make up in inherent bias. These boilerplate judgments have a history of pigeonholing entire races and genders, and in doing so they both launch and legitimize unjust operating systems throughout businesses and personal arenas worldwide. Simply put, stereotypes are where discrimination goes to breed.

Even if you don't personally subscribe to stereotyping, by living in a world that perpetuates it, you can't help but subconsciously soak up a certain amount of its stink. Think of it as ignorance by osmosis. These implanted perceptions start to influence personal decisions, not only in how we see others but also in how we see ourselves. Let's look at a well-known gender stereotype: men are born leaders. The subtext is that women are not born leaders. And it's been proven time and again that, at a very young age, children are soaking this stereotype-driven message up. In a recent study, when asked to draw a picture of a political leader, a majority of girls drew people with masculine traits.[3] Fast forward to adulthood. Women in elected office in the United States make up only 31 percent of statehouses and less than 27 percent of Congress.[4] And the internal mind screw extends far beyond the political arena. Studies show that while men are willing to apply for jobs when

---

3   College of Wooster: What Happens When You Ask a Child to "Draw a Political Leader"?

4   Rutgers: Women in State Legislatures 2023.

they meet only 60 percent of the requirements, women won't apply for that same job unless they feel 100 percent qualified.[5]

That isn't just a bias issue—that's a confidence issue. Since girls aren't inherently born without confidence, it's fair to assume that females develop an inferiority complex along the way. And this is, in no small part, informed by leadership stereotyping. Successfully internalizing a leadership mentality is crippled by the stereotypes baked into the labels we wear. Inherent bias becomes self-limiting bias when we, as humans, take it in and, somewhere in our subconscious, start to believe it's true.

Stereotypes operate in surround sound, meaning their noise is multidirectional, moving across multiple channels at once. Biases move across the outward channel of cultural conversation but also across the inward channel of personal dialogue, pushing damaging perspectives both into the world and also inward, subversively crippling our ability to change the world from the inside out.

Nobody is immune. We have all been born into the biases that stereotyping creates. They feel natural because you have always known them. But the truth is they aren't an innate part of you. You didn't come up with them—you inherited them. Stereotypes and the judgments they breed predate you by centuries. They are the product of years of inbred decisions that some small-minded people made a very long time ago. They're belief systems that grew because parents passed them down, institutions indoctrinated them (and promoted violators within their ranks), history recorded them, media perpetuated them, movie screens glorified and monetized them, and institutions far and wide accepted them.

Children are spoon-fed these thoughts and beliefs. During our most vulnerable stage of life, we are told what to believe and indoctrinated into worldviews that serve the purposes of a select few. And that, my friends, is the very definition of brainwashing. Sounds extreme, right? I agree. But stay with me because this meets all the criteria for toxic indoctrination.

Brainwashing is a systemic influencing of thought in order to get someone to adopt certain beliefs that aren't their own. When an adult joins a cult, brainwashing breaks down personal identity in order to instill group beliefs. But when we are born into these operating systems, there is no need to break down our identity because it hasn't been created yet. Instead, it is created for us by the unbendable belief systems around us.

---

5   Harvard Business Review: Why Women Don't Apply for Jobs Unless They're 100% Qualified.

Racism is systematic, as is bigotry, misogyny, homophobia, and transphobia. Every form of discrimination being fought on the front lines of equality and kindness can be traced back to these systematic belief systems that, like it or not, we were all indoctrinated into by our cultures. We aren't born believing we are better than one another—it's taught—which means it's something we have to unlearn.

TAKING THE CULT OUT OF CULTURE

It is strange to think that being a part of popular culture means admitting to being at least a little bit brainwashed. Brainwashing is something we associate with cults, which have always been considered fringe elements of our society. But the truth is, through the use of labels and stereotyping, brainwashing is very much alive and acceptably used in the heart of our society as well. The difference is perception. With cults, we consider the practice of indoctrination sinister, but with accepted institutions, we consider it tradition.

All of us are a part of something: a family, religion, club, company, political party, circle of friends, or some sort of group that adheres to a certain set of beliefs, norms, or traditions. And that's A-OK—being part of a team is a good thing. Unless that team has a problem with you thinking for yourself. Then it's time to see the red flags. When any given group expects you to never question beliefs and to toe the party line or pay the price, that's cult behavior. Being disowned by your family, banished from your community, or shamed by your peers all qualify as examples of "paying the price." Undermining your personal beliefs for the sake of group beliefs is mental subterfuge at its finest.

Setting your own personal thoughts and beliefs aside for group mind is rewarded in our world. We call that faith, loyalty, and following tradition. But here's the thing: If you aren't honoring your true beliefs as an individual, you aren't being faithful to yourself. If you aren't standing by your personal values, you aren't being loyal to your own spirit. And if you're following traditions that support a world you don't ultimately want to live in, then you are a part of the problem and not the solution.

When we stop drinking the Kool-Aid of preexisting beliefs, we can step out of systemic bias. And the sad truth is that's going to ruffle the feathers of those who are benefitting from the power of manipulating mass thinking. There are those who profit from making you feel small and therefore will convince you to buy all manner of products that will translate into bloated quarterly bonuses. There are those who gain from stirring up fear, which will make you feel threatened and willing to vote for anyone who convinces you they can make that threat go away. There are those who profit from using stereotypes to perpetuate the divisive nature of our world, thus stopping us from coming together and changing the systems that work in favor of only a select few.

So many of the labels in our world carry hidden agendas cloaked in clever salesmanship. Once you realize what that agenda is, you will have the vantage point from which to stop being manipulated by the propaganda. So, here's a worthy exercise: Interrupt the regularly scheduled programming in your head and examine some of the beliefs you live by. Ask yourself where they come from. If they didn't come from personal experience, then they aren't of your own making. If you've inherited them, regardless of the source, you have the right to question those beliefs and decide if they truly belong in your life.

Nobody has the right to make decisions for you, pit you against your fellow man, or capitalize on pain for personal gain. The wealth of the few at the expense of the many is a played-out way of life. And unraveling the labels that have long supported it is an essential step in dismantling the divisive power structure that has thrived through it. Which leads me to my next point.

THE THIRD FIB

The third not-so-little white lie that labels try to pass off as truth is that there are only two kinds of people in the world: us and them. With any given label there are those who fit within its scope and those who don't. By way of example there are those who are beautiful and those who are not. Those who are hippies and those who are not. Those who were born in this country and those who were not. And sure, on an observational level, there is inherent truth in these things. But there is inherent quicksand as well. Because looking at the world in this way focuses on our differences rather than our commonalities, which ever so subtly creates a mindset of separation. It's segregation at its most fundamental, and whether intentional or not, it undermines our sense of unity.

Operating like little clique-makers, labels divide our world. They split us into faction after faction, lessening our personal and collective power with every divide. Just as compartmentalizing who you are as an individual reduces how much of yourself you can bring to any relationship or endeavor, compartmentalizing ourselves as an entire race lessens what we can accomplish as a whole.

Defining ourselves by what makes us different from one another is not only counterproductive, it's counterintuitive. No two people are the same, so if you think about it, the fact that we are different is the one thing we all have in common. Being different from one another is not the same as being separate from one another. Differences are a reality. Separation is perception. We can be different and still work side by side. But when we start to perceive the differences between us as inferior or superior, we shift from "us and them" to "us versus them." Versus: it's a loaded little word. Place those two little syllables in between any two people or groups and, poof, opposing sides are created. It turns division into divisiveness.

They might sound the same, but there is a difference between "division" and "divisiveness." Division doesn't have to be divisive. It can simply be a tool—a means of separating something into parts. For example, business divisions organize companies into teams that specialize in particular abilities and common goals. At the base level, divisions do what labels do—create categories we can organize ourselves around.

Divisiveness is another matter entirely. It's a tool of destruction that's intentionally deployed to pit people against one another. Its whole point is to create conflict, alienation, and estrangement. Why? Because this weakens the whole and stirs up chaos, making it easier to drive a personal agenda like getting you to spend money or vote in a particular way. Whatever it is, you can trust that when divisiveness is deployed, somebody or lots of somebodies are trying to weaken or distract you in order for some sort of personal gain. The hidden motive isn't what's important; the backstage manipulation is.

Let's look a little closer at the ways labels are used to subconsciously manipulate you into an "us and them" mentality. If a brand tells you that injecting its fillers into your face will keep you looking young, what it's really saying is that you need to avoid growing old. If a political party is encouraging you to embrace one-size-fits-all family values, what it's really saying is to reject those who don't love like you do. Such messages not only trigger divisiveness between groups of people but nudge you into over associating with labels like "young" and "conservative." And this attachment makes you vulnerable to deception and manipulation because the brand or political party now holds the key to giving you what they've convinced you you need.

When we allow labels to focus us on what divides us, they germinate an adversarial nature into the fiber of our existence, which sets us up for competition rather than collaboration. As a result, we become so distracted trying to best one another, we don't even realize there is a larger agenda at play that's besting us all. Nobody has the right to treat you like a pawn on their own personal game board.

People working in different divisions of a company are still on the same team, right? Ultimately all striving for the same common goal, which is the growth and success of the overarching mission. If any division is falling behind, this threatens overall success. Well, extrapolate that out to life. The planet is one big company.

And we are all in the business of living, with a mission to do that as happily and securely as possible. But at the moment, far too many divisions of humanity are falling behind because of the damage that divisive economics, politics, and societal norms has created.

The truth is, there are no "sides" in this world. There is, ultimately, only one team. Team humanity. And there is only one world. We share the same land. We breathe the same air. We depend on the same water. We all need the same resources to survive, and therefore our well-being depends on one another.

We will always be strongest when we are cohesive. If we are going to live in an inclusive world, we need to stop holding divisive mindsets and start recognizing the things that are tearing us apart. There are so many sneaky and subliminal messages zinging around that reinforce the belief that we need to protect our own and let others fend for themselves. Nothing could be further from the truth. There is no "us" and "them." There is only "we."

CHAPTER 2

Weaponizing the Need to Belong

You only need to watch a few seconds of the news on any given day to be reminded that society is certifiably bananas. And navigating this world with any sort of integrity is no easy task. But here's some good news: hiding in between all the ups, downs, and spin-you-arounds, there's one particular moment that makes all the madness worthwhile. It looks different for each of us. It sounds different for each of us. But it sure does feel the same. I'm talking about that totally unexpected moment when you happen upon a person or a place and suddenly, instantly, magically, you feel like you're home. Familiarity. Connection. A deep and abiding sense that you've found your place in this world. I hope you know what I'm talking about because it's something we all deserve to feel. It's called *belonging*. And it's our deepest human need.

From the moment we're born, we reach out in search of arms to hold us close. Literally, with breath one, the instinct for human connection kicks in. And from that moment on, it never goes away. Throughout our lives we continue, like human heat-seeking missiles, searching out the warmth that comes from feeling loved and accepted. In psychology circles the need to belong ranks right up there with the need for food and shelter. In other words, it's required for survival.

I'm not just talking about emotional survival. Belonging is hardwired into our physical preservation as well—it's classic pack mentality, like tribes of people, herds of animals, and schools of fish. We all gather in groups because, as the saying goes, there's safety in numbers. If you're a lone wolf or an outlier, you're more susceptible to attack. When predators strike, they usually do so by singling out their target and luring them away from the group.

Be it emotional or physical, the simple truth is that buried deep in our human psychology there is a rock-solid belief that it's not safe to go it alone. This is our shared, human vulnerability. And vulnerability, in the wrong hands, can be a dangerous thing. There are those who would, and do, use it to their advantage. Because the need to belong is an intrinsic human motivator—it makes for a perfect manipulator.

This human desire is manipulated all the time in the branding world. We advertisers created bright, shiny universes of beautiful people. Painted them in an irresistible light—the perfect bodies, the coolest cars, the hippest wardrobes. We showed you a world in which money was no object, youth was eternal, and love was easy to find. Then we did our damnedest to convince you that if you bought into the labels we were selling—drank the right beer, ate the right cereal, or slathered your face with the right potions—you could be a part of this beautiful world.

In other words, we triggered your need to belong. We tapped into the "us and them" lie that labels activate and made you feel like you wanted to be a part of the tragically hip and eternally beautiful us. And we did it effectively enough to get you to think nothing of paying $300 for a pair of sneakers that cost $12 to make or dragging yourself out of bed at 4:00 a.m. to stand in line for hours to get the latest and greatest gadget du jour. Stirring subconscious desire person by person, collectively we padded the deep, deep pockets of all sorts of brands. Trust me: weaponizing belonging in the name of gain works. And not just for advertising.

Organizations worldwide use membership as a means of manipulation. There's a reason the greatest punishment an institution can dole out is abandonment: religions threaten excommunication; nations revoke citizenship; prisons enforce solitary confinement; families disown members. These are all examples of stripping us of our tribe. And in each instance your intrinsic need is being weaponized in an attempt to control you. The mere threat of being cast out is enough to get most of us to toe the line.

There is only one reason for manipulation, and that's to get something. In the case of consumerism, there's a boardroom with billionaires who want you to buy a product. In the case of political parties, there's a group of politicians who want your vote. In the case of religion, there is a governing body that wants your tithe and the promise that the next generation will be added to its ranks. There is always a motive, and it's usually focused on the benefit of the few at the expense of the many. Until we, as a human race, wake up to the hidden manipulation that's at play within the organizational labels we choose, we will continue to be pawns on someone else's chessboard.

DON'T LET YOUR NEED TO BELONG
TURN YOU INTO A BELONGING

If you're able to truly express who you are without feeling threatened by your tribe, then you belong *with* that group. If not, then you belong *to* that group. Little words. Big difference. Belonging *with* a group creates a sense of connection. Belonging *to* a group creates a system of control. Certainly, we are best when we are together. And we are happiest when we are surrounded by love and support. But if you are being asked to conform in order to fit in, you're not really being supported. And if you're being threatened with abandonment for being yourself, you aren't really being loved. You're being emotionally blackmailed.

There is no greater privilege than to be able to express and celebrate who you are and what you have to offer. It's the whole reason each of us came into the world. We are born to be self-directed human beings, but more often than not we are group-directed instead. When the balance tips, and group identity begins to override personal individuality, whether you know it or not you've entered into a transactional arrangement. The currency is belonging. What you've paid for is autonomy. A system outside yourself now has the power to call some pretty important shots in your life.

For instance, in order to wear the label of "Catholic," a person must give up their right to choose. In order to be accepted by a certain gang, a person might have to take part in violent initiations even though they hate the idea of it. In order to be a card-carrying Conservative, you are expected to stand in judgment of choices that aren't heteronormative. The list goes on and it's endless.

There are countless ways we are potentially disloyal to ourselves in order to remain loyal to a group that provides us with a sense of belonging. The underlying psychology tells us that conforming is safe while being true to yourself is dangerous. Whether we derive our sense of tribe from family, friends, work colleagues, sports teams, gaming communities, religious institutions, political affiliations, or knitting circles, the dynamic is the same. As soon as we feel there is a chance of being locked out of these circles of safety, our subconscious self-preservation kicks in and we back down on what we want and double down on whatever is required in order to continue to fit in.

Maybe that means holding back parts of who you are for fear of being disowned or rejected or turning a blind eye to others' bad behavior for fear of being ostracized or fired. Maybe it looks like refusing to leave an unhappy relationship because your family or your faith frowns upon such actions. It's often a split, subconscious decision, but every time you make it, you're telling your most authentic self that it isn't the priority in your life.

Of course, if the values and norms of the group are genuinely a reflection of your personal truths, and the label fits, then by all means, wear it. You've truly found your tribe. But if you're sacrificing any part of your individual truth in order to belong to the label the group carries, the price of belonging is too high. The cost of watering down your unique individuality to live as a generic version of yourself will eventually bankrupt your spirit.

There are a few really effective tactics that keep mass manipulation alive and well. One is the use of psychological superiority. We are told that our chosen institutions are better: Our God is the one, true God. Our way of governing is a beacon for the world. Our brand is the hottest. Our clique is the coolest. Statements like these are not only untrue, but they're divisive. The organizations making these claims use their chosen labels to activate the third cardinal lie—deliberately dividing us into camps of us and them. Across the board, be wary of a belief system that sows seeds of superiority and division. Every time we further divide ourselves by labels, we lose power. We become further and further removed from feeling like we, as a human race, belong together.

Let's take governments as an example. From birth, we are labeled as members of the countries we're born in. And with those labels we each inherit a set of national values that are drilled into us. At home, in school, and on every media channel, we're taught that our particular way of life and set of values is superior to others in the world. Then comes the interpretation of those values. This is where the labels split into political parties.

Suddenly, we aren't just letting our nationalized labels divide us by borders, but we're letting them separate us within those borders as well. If you want to be accepted as a Conservative, then you need to turn your back on liberalism and those who embrace it. If you are loyal to the cause you will vote to annihilate them. Conversely, if you are *truly* a Liberal, then your duty is to toe the party line and adopt the belief that Conservatives are greedy, money-grubbing, self-serving humans who do not care about those less fortunate. Even though those very people are also citizens of your country, the respective political party is now manipulating you to see the opposition as the enemy.

Each side, with its conflicting ideology, is certain that their way is right. From this place of infused superiority, we are manipulated to vote certain ways, donate certain amounts of money, and even, in extreme circumstances, partake in attacking churches, clinics, and as we have seen, the very government nationalism has taught us to love above all else.

The irony of this all is that if you can step out of the "story" you were born into, you'll realize that the fundamental beliefs driving nationality are completely arbitrary. People born and raised in the United States, Canada, France, Russia, Australia, China, Israel, pretty much every country, are all raised to believe that their national ideals are the best. If any of us had been born in a different country, our core fundamental beliefs would be different. And that's because the *belief* is tied to the label, not the humans wearing it.

Don't get me wrong, I wear the label of "American" proudly. I'm profoundly grateful for the opportunity and freedom it provides me. But I won't allow patriotism to lead me by the nose. My government is not infallible. And my political party is not without an agenda. It is my inalienable right and patriotic duty to question the powers that be and remain the ultimate authority in my life. And you in your life too.

We aren't just national citizens, we're global citizens, which is the most unifying label we can wear because living on this planet is something we all share. It's universal and places us all on undisputable common ground. As citizens of the globe, our loyalty belongs to all people equally. There is room to accept and help others, to live in a way that protects all of us, not just some of us.

I'm not suggesting we rebel. I'm suggesting we unite. As humans, we need to collectively open our eyes and see who and what is triggering our need to belong. As one, we need to find a way to take our autonomy back from those who stand to gain from dividing us so that we can find a more effective way to come together. When we do that we create our own sense of belonging—our own human tribe. We take back the power. Our cultural institutions have been outplaying us for so long that we've forgotten how powerful we truly are.

As individuals, we hold the actual power of any given organization or cultural system. Collectively, we wield that power. If we stopped buying products that hurt the planet, they would stop being made. If we stopped voting for people who profit from elitism, it would crumble into oblivion. If we walked away from religious institutions, maybe they would fade away, but God would still exist. A democratic society can be built without pledging ourselves to one political party. It's possible to be true to any given relationship without betraying ourselves. The trick is learning to connect with one another directly, without the labels. And to forge this deeper connection to one another, you first need to find a deeper connection within yourself.

THE GREAT DIVIDE ISN'T BETWEEN US; IT'S WITHIN US

As a human race we have become alarmingly disconnected from our innate individual wisdom. In turn, this has disconnected us from our shared collective truth. How else can we possibly explain having created a world that values products more than people and profits more than the planet? If we hadn't lost vital human connection, a great many of us would feel how wrong living like this is. But as it stands, such is not the case. We've all put so much focus on finding and building our own little tribes that we've lost sight of the fact that we were born into a much bigger tribe—the human race—and the only requirement for belonging is breathing.

Overidentifying with the labels we wear doesn't just divide us from one another, it disconnects us from ourselves. Once you start relying on external voices telling you what's right and wrong or true and untrue, you stop listening to your inner voice. And in doing so, you disconnect from an essential part of yourself. When you're separated from who you truly are, you can't meaningfully connect to anyone else. In this way, internal divisiveness leads to external divisiveness.

In addition to the societal problems this creates, there are all sorts of personal challenges that unfold as a result of living life separate from your inner wisdom. Not the least of which is this: you abandon your ability to exercise discernment. Discernment is the ability to access and operate from personal truth, and, from that place, assess the intentions of individuals and the outcomes of potential actions. Personal discernment, and the level of insight it brings with it, is one of the most incredible gifts you have been given to navigate this existence.

We live in a dishonest world that's filled with fake news and hidden agendas. It can be hard to know who to trust, which makes it all that much more important to learn to trust yourself. When you are dialed into your own truth, it's pretty hard for someone to gaslight you or emotionally blackmail you. Discernment will help you recognize labels and how they are being used both for and against you. It will teach you how, when, and which labels serve you; when you've truly found your tribe; and where you are selling off important parts of yourself, perhaps without even realizing it.

Discernment connects your human brain to your higher mind. In melding the human perspective with the spiritual understanding, you develop a well of wisdom and insight to draw from. Personal insight is the gateway to a truly unique perspective in the world. It opens you up to big-picture thinking that's on a whole new level. It's like seeing a chessboard from above rather than from the perspective of one of the pieces on the board. You access the overarching picture rather than from the limited view of what is directly in front of you.

I am not talking about intuition, which is defined as the sense of "knowing." Intuition provides a vague and somewhat general notion as to what is occurring in the unseen. Insight is a step beyond intuition and defined as "clearly seeing." Insight picks up where intuition leaves off. Insight, when properly cultivated, is the ability to parlay that vague sense into clear, understandable, actionable information.

While intuition taps into information that's available in the ethers, insight generates it from within. Ideas are ascertained, not received. Take a closer look at the word "ascertain." Break it apart and you find two words: "as certain." This level of information doesn't need to be incorporated or integrated. It's already truth—your truth.

Developing genuine personal insight requires all three of your brains operating in synchronicity. Yes, you read that right. You actually have three brains: one in your head, one in your heart, and one in your gut.

Modern science will now gladly tell you that you have a second "brain" that's found in your stomach. It's called the enteric nervous system, and it's made up of more than a hundred million neurons lining your gastrointestinal tract. While this second brain doesn't generate thought, it communicates with the brain in your head, sending signals that we interpret as instinct. Or, as we've long been calling it, gut instinct. These signals are instant and usually incredibly accurate.

But there's a middleman that stands to interfere with the signals the gut brain sends to the head brain. It's the little brain in your heart known as the intracardiac nervous system. Much like the brain in your gut, the one in your heart is not cognitive in nature. It operates by sending signals as well. But, unlike the gut instinct, your heart brain is impacted by emotion. Which means the signals it sends can be skewed by your emotional state. Feelings like anxiety and upset can interfere with communication and distort the message. This means emotional intelligence is required in order to develop the level of personal insight I'm talking about. Being mindful of your feelings rather than swept up by them will help guide you as to when you are and aren't receiving clear signals from your heart. When you're feeling out of whack, take a pause with the thoughts in your head. They are most likely a result of false signals being sent by your heart.

Stepping into a place where the heart's wisdom, the mind's intelligence, and the knowing in your gut operate in unity is a moment of human upleveling. You will have then managed to hear and trust your own quiet voice, the leader within, rather than heed the voices of the leaders around you. And since the leader within is never going to create a world that cuts you off from your fellow man, you will have found a way to protect yourself from those who would weaponize your need for belonging in order to manipulate and control you.

The only true way to find your place in this world is to first truly know who you are. By peeling back your labels and untangling yourself from group mentality, you'll be able to connect to your individuality. And there is so much more power in doing that than most people realize.

CHAPTER 3

Identity versus Individuality

I was born and identify as female—an American girl of Irish descent. I was raised in the Midwest along with my six brothers and sisters by a mom and a dad who remained married until death did they part. I am five feet, seven inches tall, was educated Catholic but as an adult, chose spirituality over religion. My hair is red, my eyes are blue, my skin is fair and freckled. I am attracted to men, allergic to gluten, and get judgy about cigarettes. I am postgraduate educated and have enjoyed an upwardly mobile career. I prefer coffee over tea, meditation over medication, and genuinely believe the magic of Harry Potter is real. I vote liberally, laugh liberally, and shop liberally. Given a choice between visiting the mountains or the beach, I would pick the mountains, hands down, every time.

There. Now you know a lot of things about me. The data is available for everyone from corporate recruiters and tourism bureaus to dating sites and political machines to decide who I am, what I want, and how they might influence me. The almighty algorithm can diversify me by race, gender, sexual preference, and socioeconomic background and auction off that information to the highest bidder. But the joke's on them. Because the truth is, none of that information defines who I *really* am. In the blink of an eye I can change most of that stuff. I can dye my hair, convert to a new religion, earn a different degree, choose to expand my sexual horizons, change my diet, jump into a new tax bracket, or switch political affiliations.

Even if I did all of those things—changed all my identifying factors—I would still be me. Because I am more than the sum total of the markers that identify me. And so are you.

Mistakenly, we consider identity to be who we are when, in fact, it is the outward-facing façade of our true selves. Identity is a series of labels, woven together, that paint a picture of a person. But a picture is a likeness of a person, not the actual person. Pictures, as you know, can be altered: We can make ourselves look happy even when we're not, for example. We can manipulate the angle from which we are seen to appear thinner. We can Photoshop people into the picture. We can post pictures online and buy thousands of "likes" in order to appear more influential. Pictures can be falsified and modified in countless ways to create an outward appearance that may or may not be authentic.

The same is true of your identity. You can claim to believe certain things to fit in, but maybe those beliefs don't really ring true for you. You can pretend to love someone who isn't really your type for fear of making a change, disappointing someone, or ending up alone. You can follow a professional path that forgoes your personal sense of purpose to please your parents or spouse. You can put on a happy face when you are crumbling inside to protect your vulnerability. There are a million ways in which the identity you claim might not be an entirely accurate depiction of the person you truly are.

Regardless of how much importance you currently place on your identity, if you want to tread into more meaningful levels of self and success, it's essential to realize that what you identify with is a *reflection* of who you are, but it's not actually *who* you are. To discover that level of self you'll have to dive a little deeper into that person in the mirror and unearth your individuality.

While often used interchangeably, identity and individuality are not actually the same thing. At least not entirely. Identity is what we consciously associate ourselves with—age, gender, race, nationality, and so forth. And, of course, it can go deeper than that. The ideologies we believe in, the humans we love, the job titles we carry, the diets we adhere to, the mistakes we make, the charities we support, the zip codes we live in, and all the other millions of little decisions we make then reflect out into the world, create our image. While many of these things are deeply felt, it doesn't change the fact that everything you come up with to differentiate yourself identity wise will still be pointing to the person you have been for however many years you have lived on this earth so far. It's finite. Individuality, on the other hand, is more enduring.

Individuality is your essence. It's something you are, not something you become. Your individuality is bigger than your body; it's the energy you embody. There's a world of difference between your body and what you embody. Your body is the physical you. The surface of who you are. This is reflected in what people, including yourself, can see and, in turn, translate into labels. On the other end of the spectrum, what you embody is the self. It's energetic and stems from the depths of your spiritual DNA, and it can't be seen until it's expressed. It's the unique blend of quirks, traits, talents, and passions that have always, without explanation, been a part of you. Body equates to identity. Embody equates to individuality.

As a concept it can sound pretty lofty, so let's bring it down to earth with an example. Transgender people are amazing teachers of body versus embody. The body these individuals are born into does not reflect the energy they embody. And as long as they live through their given physical identity, there is a misalignment to their deeper individual truth. Until the individuality that is embodied beneath the surface can be expressed, identity will continue to act as a false shell that hides, rather than enables, the true self.

The transgender experience has an immensely important lesson to teach all of us that far surpasses the limits of gender. It's about being true to who you are no matter what labels the world puts on you and accepting in a very real, very human way that we, as individuals, are so much more than the bodies we are born into.

Of course, the notion that we are more than our bodies is nothing new. Spirituality has been sending that message for eons. But traditionally, the more eternal aspect of ourselves has been approached like it's some sort of generic, one-size-fits-all dollop of divinity—like we're all Tootsie Pops with the same, sweet spiritual center. Nothing could be further from the truth. We are as unique energetically as we are physically.

OUR SPIRITS, LIKE OUR THUMBPRINTS, ARE ONE OF A KIND

It may be true, in the ultimate sense, that we are all one. An equally true fact is that while here on Earth, we are also 1 in 750 billion. We are individualized, made singular, not just by being in a body but also through the distinct collection of characteristics we possess for the time we are in that body. And you're here to embrace and express your seriously one-of-a-kind nature in a way that feels meaningful. But before you can embrace or express it, you have to drill down into a deeper insight of what that nature is.

Soul and spirit, like identity and individuality, aren't actually the same thing. There is Universal light (soul energy), and there is the individual expression of that light (spirit energy). Soul energy is the "one love" that people like Buddha to Bob Marley croon about. It's untouched, free of all thoughts, feelings, fears, prejudices, and other human creations. It's our shared origin, where we all begin. But when our spirits individualize from a single source and take on a body, each of us carves out a path that is expressly different than any other spirit in the Universe.

From the second we individualize, life happens. We encounter happiness and sadness, make friends and enemies, get hurt and hurt others, develop skills and relationships, undergo trials and tribulations, experience betrayal and loyalty, feel love and hate, take vows and break them—more or less live, laugh, and cry until eventually the body dies.

All of these vast and varied human experiences create clusters of thoughts, feelings, and behavioral patterns that are imprinted on what was previously a pure and untouched energetic state. Just as memories of our experiences are recorded into our brains, the energetic qualities of our experiences are recorded into our spirits, creating a completely unique, experience-driven expression of self. From that point forward we become individualized spirits—or as we are more commonly referred to—individuals.

If this is hard to wrap your head around, think of it in terms of a drop of water and the ocean. As part of the universal whole, we identify with everything much the same way a drop of water, when in the Atlantic, identifies as being the ocean. Not just a *part* of the ocean, but as the *whole* ocean. But once that drop is removed from the whole, it can become all kinds of different things. It can be a raindrop that experiences what it feels like to sail through the air. It can become filtered drinking water and discover what it's like to be bottled, carted in a backpack, and gulped down a throat to hydrate a human. It can be added to a recipe and become part of a meal. It can be frozen and fluffed into a snowflake. It can be sprayed from a sprinkler, the impetus of a small child's giggle on a hot summer day. The possibilities for that drop of water, once it leaves the ocean, are endless.

And so it is with each of us. From the time you first ventured from the all-encompassing ocean of energy, you've been accumulating unique experiences and perspectives, both positive and negative in nature. Your individuality is defined by the unique collection of traits, talents, passions, and proclivities that you have curated via the unique experiences you have lived. This includes not only your strengths but your shortcomings. We all have energetic wounds to heal, debts to pay, and life lessons to learn. These, too, are a part of our individualized expressions, and none of them relies on identity markers such as skin color, the designation of anatomical parts, or country of origin. The only thing that influences these gifts of individuality is the degree to which you acknowledge or ignore them.

To give an example, I was born with the ability to write. It's been a part of me from the start. I began being paid for it in the sixth grade. Writing is a gift, not a label. It comes from the deepest parts of who I am, and I feel most at peace and authentic when expressing myself through this deep-seated ability. I'd be a writer regardless of my anatomy, nationality, sexual preference, or any other identity label. I am on this planet, at least in part, to grow this talent and share myself with the world in doing so, regardless of the circumstances surrounding me. I could have been born a six-toed man in Timbuktu, and I still would have been born a writer.

You, too, have deeper gifts. It's important to understand where they stem from and why they matter. Doing so holds the power to amp up your success quotient in two critical areas: First, it will ignite genuine passion that will do wonders for your performance. Second, it will activate a sense of purpose that you aren't going to find anywhere else, thus bringing deeper meaning and sense of personal fulfillment.

So many people are searching for purpose. We turn to our careers, our relationships, and our families to provide us with the meaning that feels lacking in our lives. This will never fully cut the mustard, because if you're looking outside yourself for your life's purpose, then you are looking in the wrong place. There is a saying that goes something akin to, "The only Zen you find on a mountain top is the Zen you bring with you." Similarly, the only true sense of purpose you find in a career or relationship is the purpose you bring. You have to find it in yourself first, then you can experience it in the world around you.

Purpose comes from within your individuality. Expressing your essential self—the personal talents and truths that are housed within your individual nature—is literally your reason for being. When you find a way to give to your work at this level, you will get from your work in equal measure. What could be more purposeful or passion-driven than being the person you came here to be?

Now, on to performance. A more practical ancillary benefit of bringing your individual gifts into the mix is that they give you a competitive edge. If there is one thing that's going to help you succeed above all others, it's learning to lead from your personal strengths. And ground zero for personal strengths is individuality.

The things you naturally excel at stand to be the greatest business advantage you could possibly have. It seems strange to say, but a vast majority of people don't know the full extent of their personal strengths. So many of our unique abilities end up being overlooked or cast aside because we live in a world that doesn't always value them. As a result, millions of people begin believing at an early age that the things that make them unique are different than the things that can help them succeed. Consequently, individuality is often put on the back shelf of life, where it collects dust and does you no good. When you compartmentalize yourself like this, you're leaving money on the table. With a little creative repurposing, your natural inclinations can be brought into any job to increase passion and improve performance.

By way of example, let's say you were born with a flair for the dramatic and love acting. As a kid, you sang into your hairbrush on a daily basis and auditioned for every play in middle school and high school. But then, graduation rolled around, and you came to a crossroads in life. The world said that it was time to "grow up." And since the odds of becoming a successful actor were steep, you decided to set that love aside and pursue a more stable path. You still see every movie released and buy season tickets to the theater to feed your passion, but you've relegated yourself to the role of spectator, leaving your gift on the sidelines of your life.

Here's the thing: actors are born performers, which is a skill that can lend itself to all kinds of productive applications, like being a great presenter in a boardroom. How can leaning into that not serve you well in your professional development? Trust me, I've witnessed plenty of bad ideas get sold thanks to good presentation skills (think of those terrible TV commercials that you've watched throughout the years.) Another example is gardening. If you were born with a green thumb, that means you can cultivate growth. I defy you to name a company in existence that doesn't value growth.

The parallels between personal strengths and professional performance always exist. But identifying and, in turn, leveraging them to your advantage can only happen if you stop sidelining the attributes of your individuality and start utilizing them. So, stop listening to the voices around and inside of you that have a prefab, cookie-cutter plan for what it means to be a grown-up.

Casting aside your gifts and truths because it is the safe thing to do is a crime against humanity—*your* humanity. It does you no good to put your individual talents and passions aside in the name of being a "responsible adult." There's nothing random about the talents and traits you were born with. They're a part of your operating system and exist to help you become the best version of yourself. Turning your back on that is one of the most irresponsible things you can do.

In fact, if we really wanted to get granular about it, take a good, close look at the word "responsibility." It's really two words—"response" and "ability"—shoved together. Hidden right there, in plain sight, is a way more empowering way to look at what it means to be responsible. Living responsibly means living in a way that enables you to *respond* to your *abilities*.

If the mainstream educational paths laid out before you don't allow you to utilize your gifts and abilities, then chart your own course. If the job description you are working within doesn't let you do that, expand it. We live in a world where entrepreneurial and intrapreneurial efforts are celebrated. Innovation reigns supreme across all industries. There's a bigger jackpot than ever waiting for you if you dig deeper into understanding and leveraging your individuality, which also happens to be just good common sense. If you leverage the things that you're naturally good at, you're going to perform well.

If you trust one thing in this world, let it be yourself. Know, with unrelenting certainty, that you embody specific abilities and oddball quirks for a reason. The elements of your individuality—those unique traits, talents, skills, passions, and perspectives—can be combined into a platform that has the power to launch you into the success you are looking for in your life. You can spend your life second-guessing them or you can spend it using them.

Labeling any of your abilities as monetarily worthless or your personal passions as impractical childhood dreams doesn't just cloud your individuality but disables it. Doing so gives you permission to quit on key parts of yourself. And the sad thing about that is, more often than not, you do so with the blessing of the world around you. It's challenging to live in a culture that doesn't champion individuality. Our world makes it very easy to ignore that which makes you unique in order to embrace that which lets you belong.

The time has come for us to start having a little more faith in who we intrinsically are. There is a reason you have the interests and passions you do. Trust that the part of you that holds your truths knows what it's doing. Just because a given path might be impractical doesn't mean it isn't valuable. Casting aside the passion with the path is like throwing out the baby with the bathwater. Passion is bigger than any one path. It doesn't care how you employ it, It only cares that, in one way or another, you bring it into the light of day and ride it for all it's worth.

Passion's superpower is that it's unreasonable. It's an emotional force that refuses to relent in the face of adversity. Which means that just because you set it aside doesn't mean it will go away. Ignored passion festers. It creates toxic feelings toward our bosses, our career paths and ourselves. When we don't find a way to express who we are in the lives we lead, and our careers are a major part of those lives, it generates a deep sense of unease and dissatisfaction. It's no wonder that poll after poll reports nearly half of the global workforce is unhappy in their jobs.

Tapping into your individuality enables you to sidestep that kind of unhappiness. Passion and purpose are intrinsic indicators of who you truly are. They are the rewards for openly sharing what you, uniquely, have brought to the table of Life. Doing so might be frightening, inconvenient, or a total grind at times. But even so, it will always beat the alternative, which is being herded along by our culture of conformity.

If you don't decide how you want to live your life, trust me, someone else will decide for you. Maybe it will be your parents, and then you follow their path because it's what you know but not necessarily what you love. Maybe it will be your own fears that tell you your passion is nothing but a pipe dream, and you aren't good enough, or deserving enough, to have a life that makes you seriously happy. Maybe it will be our cultural falsehood that says living and making a living are two separate things and you have no right to expect to find meaning in both.

There is no shortage of people in the world with opinions, both welcome and unwelcome, who will always believe they know what's best for you. And while we all need advice and guidance now and then, it's time to trust the voice within over the voices that surround. Being your true self requires turning down the volume of all the outside influences that try to tell you the right and wrong way to live and tune into the wisdom of individuality. The truth is you are the one and only person who will ever exist inside your skin. You're the only one who really knows what it feels like to live with the decisions *you* make.

So, how do you reset the boundaries of limiting labels and other outside influences? That answer is simple: boss up.

YOU ARE THE CEO OF YOUR LIFE

Running a life is not that much different than running a business. The Universe is like a giant holding company. Since we have all borrowed a little of its stardust in order to create our own existence, it holds shares in each of us. We, as individual expressions within that shareholder's portfolio, are subsidiary brands; independent operators within the overarching structure who have the ability to maintain our own identity and operate autonomously, conducting this business of Life according to our own set of bylaws.

In other words, each of us is our own company within the parent company. Inside that structure, you are the sole proprietor, designated to lead your personal enterprise from beginning to end. As such, you are no low-level executive. You are the head honcho. As the CEO, it is your job to grow your assets and use what you've got to profit the world. The Universe is expecting a dividend of positive energy the next time you appear in front of its board members.

The way this is done personally is the same as the way it's done professionally. First, take inventory. What do you have to offer? Dig deep into your individuality and take stock of what is on its shelves, meaning your talents, passions, traits, and anything else that makes up your unique value. You have to know what you have before you can find a way to offer it.

Once you have taken stock of your inventory, create your product. How will you put your raw materials together to make an offering that "profits" (i.e., benefits) both you and the world you live in? From there, define your market. Where, from industry to social circles, will the valuable product known as *you* be in demand and make the most impact? What groups of people need your brand of being?

Having determined your market, now develop your marketing. How are you going to reach these people you know you have the power to help? A little heads-up here: this is where you are going to have to push beyond your own insecurities and learn how to talk about yourself clearly and confidently. If you don't buy what you're selling, no one else will either.

With these pieces in place, you now have to do what every CEO on the planet has to—grow the company. This requires good management, which means instilling a few best practices, one of which is budgeting—and not just your money but all of your resources. As humans, our most valuable assets beyond our individual strengths include our health, our time, and each other. The way a vast many run their lives, these areas of life end up getting little attention beyond the tattered bits of energy left in reserve at the end of each day. This isn't sustainable and calls for the reallocation of your resources. The key word in the term balance sheet is "balance."

Rebalancing occasionally requires a reorg. Sometimes, people in your life are comfortable with your identity but not your individuality. They don't want you to grow and change. But your individuality is ground zero for personal innovation, and living from that place means continuous growth and change. When you start leveraging your originality, you stop living like a data point in someone else's algorithm, and that changes the game. If there are people in your life who don't like the new game, it's not appropriate to force them to play. Nobody wins when you try to force your past into your future. It's by no means a fun part of the job, but every CEO has to learn how to let people go. It's a scary concept for sure, and if the day comes that you find yourself confronted with the need to restructure your inner circle, do what all leaders do. Take it slow. Make a plan. And always, always, execute with humanity.

Of course, I don't wish that for you. My hope is that your life is filled with courageous spirits who want to continually pioneer new frontiers right along with you. We all need people who are willing to live beneath the surface and are excited, not threatened, by growth. Because every great company needs to innovate to remain relevant. Individuality breeds innovation and ensures that you never cave to the pressures of conformity. Because the cost of doing that is far too high.

CHAPTER 4

The Cost of Conformity

In ancient China, there was a common practice called foot-binding. Somebody somewhere got it in their heads that small feet were erotic and subsequently, women who had them were more desirable. As a result, young girls were put through excruciating pain in order to try and fit this norm. Around the age of four or five, their feet would be bound in order to try and keep them from growing.

Here's how that process went: All but the big toe would be turned under the sole of the foot and then cloth strips would be wrapped tightly around the toes to keep them in place. As the bones did what they're supposed to do—grow—there would be no room for the toes to expand. Over the course of years, the foot would break over and over and the arch would often be destroyed completely. These poor little girls would have to delicately hobble through their lives, taking tiny steps if they could walk at all. As a result of being forced to conform to somebody else's notion of who they should be, countless women were put through excruciating pain and lost the ability to walk through their own lives easily and freely.

I use this as an example, albeit an extreme one, of what can happen when we allow the world to mold us into a socially acceptable version of ourselves. Conformity, the act of watering down our quirks, silencing our perspectives, and adapting our gifts in the name of fitting in, binds our spirit from expressing naturally. When you conform, you stunt your personal growth and position yourself to have to hobble through life as less than you were born to be. Conformity camouflages true nature. It's a spectacular form of self-sabotage.

From the earliest ages, we make decisions based on who we think we need to be to fit in. We get to the playground and, because we want to be liked and included, we start to minimize and hide behaviors we fear will land us on the wrong end of a joke. We get a little older and start to have crushes. Suddenly, we are dressing and acting in ways we hope will attract that chosen person. Fast forward again, and we are on social media, expressing not who we are but who we think will get us the most likes and the most followers. Fast forward yet again, and we're choosing educational paths before we even know what we want to do because that's what the world tells us is next. From there, we step onto career paths that make us money but not necessarily happiness because that's what we're told grown-ups do. More often than not, we don't even think of such things as conforming. We think of them as socially and financially succeeding.

Spotting the million little ways in which we conform to meet outside approval is easy to miss. It's blended seamlessly into some of the most sought-after labels in our lives. I'm talking about labels like "cool" and "successful." Being considered cool gives you, for the most part, an all-access pass in social circles. It garnishes invites to the best parties, grants you access to the most elite cliques, and makes you the envy of those around you. Same for being successful. Meet society's definition of success and you can buy fancy cars, live in upscale neighborhoods, and afford lavish trips. Who doesn't want that?

A simple fact of our world is that conformity is rewarded. When we make ourselves look and act like everyone else, we are accepted socially. When we follow the respected educational paths, we are offered the better jobs. When we toe the company line, we get promoted. When we memorize what we're expected to, we get good grades. When we do as we're told, we receive praise. When we meet certain beauty standards, we are more likely to be romantically pursued. These are the carrots that are dangled to keep us focused on what's right in front of us instead of looking at the bigger picture. Which is that by conforming, we are feeding a system that holds us back.

Authentic success means bringing more of yourself to the table, not less. Not only are all your odd little quirks, unique perspectives, and passions that define your individuality your superpowers, they are your right. You have the right to be yourself and to be loved, praised, promoted, and appreciated as such. Nobody gets to tell you whether you are good enough or pretty enough to succeed in your life. Nobody gets to tell you that you are too young or too old to make a difference. Nobody gets to tell you that you are less than because of what you weigh or what color your skin is. Nobody gets to decide for you what success means or how many dollars define it. Nobody gets to decide how you need to learn, what you need to know, or whether or not your voice has value in the world. Nobody, except you, that is.

The biggest success stories in the world are all stories of people who refused to conform. Steve Jobs didn't cave to the pressure to get a bunch of fancy degrees. The Wright brothers didn't let the law of gravity keep them from flying. Ellen DeGeneres didn't let anyone force her to hide who she is. And in each instance, the lesson is the same. Bet on yourself and you stand to win big. Think about how different the world might be if any of these people caved to the status quo. The world we live in would have less creativity, less exploration, less laughter.

You, too, have an originality that can bring amazing success and make a meaningful difference to the world at large. Don't let the pressure to conform and the labels that society deems acceptable force you to hide that originality. The things that make you original will help you succeed. Holding back your unique perspectives keeps others from being able to see how insightful you really are. Setting aside your personal passions diminishes the level of dedication you can bring to your professional endeavors. Hiding your individual quirks to blend in is going to keep you from standing out. Your originality is ground zero for personal innovation. It's your essence, and therefore essential.

CONFORMITY: THE ORIGINAL(ITY) SIN

Your individuality is a gift to be celebrated, not a sin to be covered up. When it comes to human beings, there is no such thing as a parody product. We are all one of a kind, limited editions that will never come around in exactly the same way again. Yet few of us seem to operate with the understanding of how deeply valuable that truly is. When I look around, what I see is that our unique and individual natures are getting the snot beat out of them by the status quo of our world.

I saw this in the advertising world every time a piece of business was won or lost. A shift in the bottom line set a flurry of closed-door conversations in motion as people were ushered in the door, out the door, and on to new accounts that, in truth, they weren't always very well matched for. With a few exceptions, none of this was done with malice or ill intent. But even so, the subtext of the conversations and overall operating system was powered by the unspoken belief that people are interchangeable commodities that can be bought and traded for what is often an unfair market price.

In all fairness, this practice is pretty much business as usual across all business sectors. But what makes it particularly ironic in advertising is that we were in the business of originality and should have known better. It was, literally, our job to turn parody products into unique expressions. But instead, we were taking the most unique expressions on the planet–human beings–and treating them like parody products. Here we advertising elite were, elevating something as unoriginal as a cornflake onto a pedestal, all the while treating brilliant minds and one-of-a-kind humans like line items on a spreadsheet.

What is even more disturbing is watching just how willing people are to take it. The wealth of our world is so unevenly distributed that a vast majority can't run the risk of losing a paycheck, even for the briefest of times. As a result, we mold ourselves to fit into the cog of someone else's wheel for a sense of security. This operating system has resulted in a human race that, for the most part, has lost sight of how rare and valuable we are as individuals. And that's the true cost of conformity. Because if you don't value what you have to offer, nobody else is going to either. And that devaluation can translate into being overlooked for a promotion, underpaid for a position, or taken for granted in any number of ways.

Once you start acting like a common commodity, you energetically issue an invitation for others to treat you as such. Conformity sucks the originality out of us and morphs us into generic offerings. And here's the thing about generic products: the entire appeal is that they can be sold on the cheap. Why would you ever create a situation in which you, as a human being, could be bought and sold on the cheap?

Our willingness, be it conscious or not, to conform to the one-size-fits-all molds being handed out from all sides, has human beings—the most valuable and original offerings on the shelf of Life—behaving like parody products. Think about this: one-of-a-kind pieces of art sell for hundreds of millions of dollars in auction houses, while one-of-a-kind human beings regularly rent themselves out for hourly wages.

There is nothing wrong with working for an hourly wage if doing so offers you a means of expressing who you truly are and sharing your gifts with the world in a way that allows you to create a happy life. But if that isn't the case, if you find you are operating as a generic human being rather than boldly bringing your passions, perspectives, and personal gifts to the forefront of your life, then don't be surprised if you aren't happy with your earning potential. Conformity is robbing you of life's richness, both personally and professionally. It's also robbing the rest of us of the richness of a world made better by your unique contribution.

Conforming comes at a cost. Always. Both personally and professionally, you will pay in one way or another if you turn your back on what you uniquely have to offer and allow yourself to play a smaller game than you came here to play. On a personal level, when you force yourself to conform, you allow yourself to be bullied. Sounds strange, but it's true. Something you perceive as bigger or stronger than yourself (culture, economics, expectations, etc.) intimidates you into behaving in certain ways. Even when it's subliminal, being bullied creates stress and leads to low self-esteem. And nothing turns up the smack talk in your head like a lack of self-confidence.

On the professional front, conformity cuts you off at the knees because it robs you of the greatest competitive edge you are ever going to have. Despite popular opinion, your competitive advantage in the professional arena isn't your education or who you know—it's you. The individual ways in which only you can contribute are what will set you apart. You may get a job because of who you know or the pedigree on your resume, but those things aren't going to help you keep or excel in that job. That's all you.

Your innate talents and personal passions define your strengths. Your unique personality traits and personal values make you likable. Talent, passion, and likability are the trifecta of success in the business world. And conformity, which undermines the ability to believe in yourself, robs you of all three. The cost of not believing in yourself at work translates into not having the guts to ask for what you deserve. This, in turn, makes it easy for a company to pass you over for promotions or give you piddly raises that don't reflect what you can actually contribute. The bottom line: Conformity is bad for the bottom line. You end up leaving a lot of money on the table when you hold back parts of who you are.

Conversely, high self-worth can readily translate into high net worth. Because when that's the case, you don't hold back. Regardless of personal versus professional arena, when you share your truths and live from your strengths, it pays off. None of this can happen in an impactful way when you acquiesce to conforming to whom family culture, company culture or popular culture tell you to be.

To be fair, this sort of autonomous living is not easily won. Because we live in a culture that breeds conformity, people are afraid of change. So, there's one thing that you can count on when stepping out of the mainstream and into your individuality: fast feedback. People. Will. Have. Opinions. And plenty of them. Those who are not comfortable with your shift into bigger degrees of yourself will have something to say about it. You will get plenty of input about what you should and shouldn't do and why. It's always worth listening, but discernment and bravery will be the call of the day in such situations. Because "should" is a dangerous word.

In order to keep us confined to the labels we live within, conformity relies heavily on this one little word. We are convinced that we "should" look a certain way, act a certain way, follow a certain path, marry a certain person, or make a certain amount of money. The word "should" is one of the more powerful weapons in the arsenal of conformity. It holds the power to transform choice into obligation. And doing anything because you feel like you have to, rather than because you freely choose to, changes the dynamic entirely.

Labeling something as an obligation rather than an opportunity changes the way you experience it. Obligations are burdens. Seeing something or someone as a job you have to show up for makes that person or experience a heavy weight to carry. Opportunities, on the other hand, are choices. They present us with the possibility of what could be versus what should be. What "could be" is an approach that begets excitement and exploration, not guilt and obligation.

Experiencing what could be is the whole point of living. This life is an opportunity, but if it's feeling like a burden, there's a good chance you are living from a place of obligation, not possibility. And this can be exhausting. When you conform to what you feel you should do or who you feel you should be, you energetically shortchange yourself. You put less of yourself into the world. And the less you give of yourself, the less you can receive in return. This is how energy works. It orbits in circles. What you put out into the world comes back to you. So, if you dam up your personal expression by conforming to what you believe you should be, that lesser amount is what's going to come back to you. That can take the form of less money in a paycheck. It can be less happiness in your days. It can be less intimacy in a relationship where the person doesn't know who you truly are because you haven't truly shown them.

In addition to crippling your originality, living from a place of "should" robs you of your individual autonomy. Rather than letting your inner light guide you, you outsource your life's GPS to the opinions of those surrounding you. Somewhere in your psyche you've decided that others know what's best for you or have the right to decide for you. For the record, nothing could be further from the truth. There is nobody—literally nobody—in this world who will ever know what it's like to live in your skin except you. That makes you the expert in this arena. You are the only person who will ever be qualified to decide how to authentically live.

I'm not encouraging you to be a self-centered a-hole. Of course, we should all consider how our actions impact others. And certainly, there will be others—a select few who you love, trust, and admire—whose opinions and input you will value. This is a good thing, just so long as you don't appreciate the other voices more than your own. Which, in a world that has trained us to look outside ourselves for validation, is not as easy as it may sound. Labels keep us living on the surface of our lives and keep us looking outside for validation. This makes it difficult to genuinely get to know yourself. Which, in turn, makes it basically impossible to trust yourself. Without this sense of internal confidence, it's so easy to be pushed around by the world. Which is exactly what conformity does. It's the world bullying you into being the person it wants you to be, not the person you came here to be. And nothing makes the world feel more dangerous than a good bully. When facing one, it's a very natural reaction to run away and hide.

Conforming is a socially acceptable way of hiding. And when you don't feel safe being seen for who you are, a feeling of aloneness takes root, allowing a subtle sense of isolation to grow. In reaction, the desire to belong grows stronger and a greater willingness to conform kicks in with the hope of finding a way to fit in. This, in turn, distorts even greater degrees of self, which only serves to exacerbate the core problem of not truly being seen. It's a nasty little catch-22 that we, as a human race, are outgrowing.

Hiding ourselves in order to find acceptance is an outdated operating system that can't be sustained if we step up to the call of the day and evolve as human beings. We are, as a people, being asked to deepen our faith in ourselves and our faith in the ability of others to love and accept us for who we are. The unique person that you are deserves all the respect in the world. Because the person you are is not here by fluke or random accident.

A very wise part of yourself, one that supersedes the human you are being, played a central role in deciding the individual traits and gifts that you brought into this life. These unique abilities—the things that you excel at most naturally and love most deeply—are your competitive edge in this life. But guess what? They might not be the things that most help you fit in. Your talents and quirks might not meet the criteria of the cool kids. And your passions may not send you down a career path that leads to what society deems as successful. But that doesn't mean you can't have personal happiness and financial security. It just means it might look different than the status quo. Which is actually a good thing. Not only is the status quo overrated, it's, potentially, one of the greatest obstacles to your individuality.

Individuality is the archenemy of conformity. Your unique quirks, traits, and passions do the exact opposite of helping you fit in. When you water them down, you rob yourself of the chance to win in your own life. When you embrace them, good things magically unfold. When you accept and lean into what you are naturally good at, then you are naturally going to excel. If you allow personal passion to guide you, you'll never have to search for a feeling of purpose or meaning in your life. And when you show the world who you really are, you'll find people who will love you without the need for modification.

Once you accept these parts of yourself, the pressure of conforming to labels will lose power over you. It won't matter how the beauty brands say you should look, because you will already have acceptance just as you are. And it won't matter how the political machines want you to vote, because when you are living your truth, it's easy to see which candidate best represents it. And it won't matter how any given religion tells you to pray, because you will have connected with the higher individual wisdom that resides within you.

When you reach this point, you are *informing* the world of who you are, not *conforming* to who it thinks you should be. All three of the little fibs will have lost their power over you, and you will no longer be living their lie.

PART 2

A Gender Rebrand

CHAPTER 5

Gender: The First of Our Labels

We've spent a lot of time deconstructing labels and shining a light on the general degrees of toxicity they bring to our world. Now, let's get specific. Let's dive into a case study and really put the theory to the test. To do that, I invite you to jump into a time machine and take a trip back to the womb. Let's journey back to that place where you were given your first label: boy or girl. No sooner does the news arrive that a baby is on the way then the big question kicks in: *What kind* of baby is it? As newly forming beings, we only get to be neutral, expectation-free humans for a hot minute before we get slapped with a gender label, which, in turn, triggers a barrage of preset expectations and powerful dynamics that will continue to influence and impact us for the rest of our lives. The mindsets and norms surrounding gender are so tightly woven into the fabric of our culture, ideas about who we should be begin to form even before our bodies do.

Being pigeonholed before birth is a tricky thing. We are, at that point, more energy than matter. This makes us wide-open sponges of consciousness, prone to soaking up the energy of the thoughts and feelings of the one carrying us and the others surrounding us. So, when, from the get-go, we are fed ideas about what it means to be a girl and a boy, we absorb them into our newly forming systems. These culturally binary ideas of personal expression and gender norms are woven into what becomes the subconscious and then are reinforced once we are born into the world that adheres to our labels.

Once a gender label is assigned, the train of assumptions roars out of the station. Gender-reveal cakes are baked pink or blue. Closets are filled with dresses or pants. Rooms are decorated with butterflies or sports cars. Dolls are designated to one camp and baseball bats to another. On and on it goes. While all of this has long been the natural way of things and seems harmless on the surface, the truth is, it holds us back in ways we don't even fully understand. Long before we get a chance to figure out who we are as individuals, the world has made a million decisions and assumptions about who we are supposed to be. All around us are signs pointing us down one of two clearly defined and culturally accepted paths of belonging.

Because these assumptions are so hardwired into our culture, when we finally start growing up and get a sense of who we are, we find that there are costs to freely express our personal truths. If a girl would rather play sports than with dolls, she's labeled a tomboy. If a boy would rather dance than wrestle, he's labeled a sissy. In both cases, a social stigma is triggered. The person being labeled is made to feel that they aren't normal and that they have to make a choice to either hide who they are or fight the discomfort of expressing themselves. This is not a choice anyone should ever have to make.

Often, the popular opinion in such cases is that the person is going through a "phase" that will eventually be outgrown. That is an assumption dripping with condescension. When you label a girl "tomboy" and assume it's a phase she'll outgrow, you belittle her as a person. Expecting someone to simply grow out of that which brings them joy holds an unspoken admonishment that their natural way of being is juvenile and insignificant. It also makes an arrogant assumption that someone's authentic and personal expression is, in fact, somehow not the natural way of things. These unspoken opinions, no matter how subtle, are recorded by the psyche. Somewhere inside, the person feels the tug to bend their truths and become something other than who they are. And in that, a choice must be made: conform to what others think you should be or fight for who you know yourself to be. Faced with that decision over and over again, pressure starts to build. And the cumulative effect of that pressure can throw an impressionable kid off their natural path. It's crap.

Natural inclinations are not phases that a child needs to outgrow. They're early indicators of talents and passions that should be encouraged and nurtured, regardless of how they do or don't fit into cultural norms. If we want to set children up for success, we need to set aside our notions of who we think they should be and take a better look at who they actually are. Personal interests are hints from the Universe, pointing toward paths that hold happiness, purpose and passion.

Personal passions point us in the direction of personal calling. And the sooner anyone can find their way onto that path, the more readily and evidently a purpose-driven life can reveal itself. When we force kids into gender norms, no matter how subtle, we potentially—and in fairness, often unintentionally—throw them off the path they were born to follow in favor of one that is more culturally acceptable but, most likely, less authentic. Here's the deal: when it comes to what's best for an individual, nobody knows better than that person living inside that skin. Our North Star is anchored within us, not in the labels surrounding us.

As we continue to unpack the detrimental byproducts of gender labels, it's easy to see that they don't just limit us individually—they limit us collectively as well. Historically, the words "male" and "female" are as powerful a force for divisiveness as it gets. Boys and girls are brought up to believe they are on different teams—teams that are given different sets of rules and standards for behavior and success. As a result, we are positioned to live as adversaries rather than allies. Let's look at a classic example.

A LADY VERSUS A LADIES' MAN

Growing up, girls are taught to act like ladies whereas boys are taught to admire the ladies' man. The metric for success for a lady is to remain chaste. For a ladies' man it's to get a woman to engage in unchaste behavior. For one person to succeed, the other must fail. Collaboration isn't an option. Competition is the only choice. How can we ever truly be part of the same team with dynamics like this at play?

These toxic dynamics, which reinforce the divide between men and women, are everywhere. Fairy tales teach us to believe in white knights who require damsels in distress: a scenario in which men are pressured to be heroes and women taught that they can't save themselves. The divisive double standard goes on and on. Assertive men are bosses. Assertive women are bitches. Financially successful men are attractive. Financially successful women are intimidating. When women stay home to raise kids it's natural. When men stay home to raise kids it's assumed they have somehow failed or given up.

The expectations we inherit with our gender labels don't just divide us mentally, they divide us emotionally. When something distressing happens, rather than openly feel it, men are expected to man up. The unspoken rule here is that it's not enough to be strong. To be a "real man" requires suppressing all weakness. And for whatever weird reason, somewhere in our human evolution, somebody decided that showing emotion is a weakness. As a result, boys are taught to stifle and censor emotion. In the absence of learning how to skillfully handle feelings, there is discomfort with emotional displays. And since women are emotional by nature, there is, again, a divisive and dysfunctional dynamic woven into our personal interactions.

Here's the thing: if we are to stop living in a divided world, we need to embrace emotion. Feelings are the very means by which we connect to one another. And yet, instead of cultivating this, we hide our feelings from one another and talk about "catching feelings" like they're a virus or toxin. Gender labels have created a popular culture in which we act allergic to the very thing that brings us together. It's another no-win situation for creating a united world. This pattern has us all living in our heads instead of our hearts. If we could reverse that, and actually come from a place of feeling, there would be a lot more empathy and a lot less atrocity in our world.

If we could step out of certain systematic behaviors, we'd see that we've all been mass hypnotized into believing that we, as human beings, are defined by the labels we wear. But, when in a hypnotic state, we have no idea that we're being controlled by an outside influence. Everything we are doing feels totally normal. As a result, we are carrying unhealthy baggage that just gets heavier and heavier throughout time. Think of all the stereotypes and self-sabotaging mindsets you've been navigating your whole life: fight like a girl; take it like a man; a woman's place; a man's world; a girl's best friend; boys will be boys. All this misleading culturalism started with labels we were given before we even drew our first breath.

I'd like to circle back to a particular phrase in that last paragraph: boys will be boys. Because it's worth pausing on. This little gem is particularly insidious because it transforms the gender label into an excuse. And with this shift the labels aren't just dividing us, they're giving us permission to mistreat each other. Through phrases like this, boys are taught bad behavior, such as fighting, smack-talking, and objectifying, are acceptable. And the rest of us are taught to indulge such behaviors because, well, that's just the way things are. And with that violence and victimization both become normalized.

It's time to stop letting these toxic ways of being permeate our world. Using our preconceived labels as excuses to shrug off bad behavior negates any ability to own those behaviors. And until they're owned, they can't be changed. Adopting a unity consciousness isn't simply about accepting people for who they are; it's also about not accepting behaviors people engage in that hold us back from being who we can ultimately be.

A big part of the problem is that we have all come to accept the norm. The cultural labels and their corresponding belief systems and behaviors that we have tolerated for far too long have created a long-standing blind spot and this has led to biased and toxic systems. Indoctrinated patterns have created predatory tendencies and all manner of bad behaviors in both the personal and professional arenas. As a result, movements such as #Metoo and Time's Up have arisen.

These movements are so important. They mark a turning point in the unfair and unacceptable patterns that have thrived in the shadow of the collective blind eye for far too long. However, because dysfunction runs deep, the reckoning they have brought has created its own set of challenges. Fear, frustration, and uncertainty on how to interact now that the norms have been disrupted are giving rise to disturbing blowback, particularly in the professional world.

Studies show that a majority of male managers are uncomfortable interacting with their female colleagues at work. This includes being in one-on-one meetings and mentoring. It gets better. And by better, I mean worse. Twenty-one percent of men said they would be reluctant to hire a woman for a job that requires close interaction and 19 percent they would be reluctant to hire an attractive woman.[6] This is the very definition of discrimination on the basis of gender. Think about this for a second: in overreacting to the very reasonable request that we put an end to sexual harassment, we are now giving rise to sexual discrimination. That's just trading one problem for another, which, I think we can all agree, was not the point of the recent social justice movements. The idea is to create better working relationships, not more difficult ones. The dysfunction of the current dynamics at play sets everyone, both men and women and the companies they work for, up for failure.

By missing out on mentorship relationships, women's career trajectories are compromised. And the stress men experience due to uncertainty of how to interact with their female colleagues diminishes focus and productivity. When interactions are driven by fear and defensiveness, there isn't a lot of room for connection and collaboration.

In many ways, rather than bringing us closer, the demand for decency and equality has driven men and women apart. It's totally ironic. And, if you're buying into the premise of this book, totally understandable. The labels we wear and the wagons we are circling around those labels are deepening division and strengthening polarization. Not only does this growing tendency toward gender polarization threaten to disintegrate corporate culture from the inside out but it also isn't sustainable. Women comprise 47 percent of the US labor force.[7] It doesn't take a lot of common sense to realize that half of our workforce actively disengaging the other half is a recipe for a human resources disaster. It's also monumentally bad for the bottom line.

Have you ever been a part of a team that didn't know how to work together? It's draining beyond belief. The finger-pointing, frustration, and CYA antics this type of environment breeds is incredibly costly, both personally and professionally. High drama equates to low productivity. That's bad for profits. But high drama also equates to low morale. And that's bad for people. While financial capital is important, human capital is invaluable. There is nothing more valuable than living, breathing, passion-driven people who make the wheels of industry go around. Literally nothing. And the current dysfunction at play within gender labels is setting both men and women up for spectacular failure.

When we, as employees, find ourselves in a toxic work environment where we can't perform at the top of our game, we're on our way to bottoming out. By

---

6   Harvard Business Review: The #MeToo Backlash.
7   Population Reference Bureau: Record Number of Women in the US Labor Force.

not hitting the marks we are capable of, we get passed over for promotions and bonuses. This results in resentment and feeling devalued and underappreciated, which, in turn, breeds disengagement—generating even more division within the ranks. The trickle-down effect of our widening gender camps makes us disengaged from both the people we work with and the work we do.

Success requires a sense of connection —connection to what we are doing and to the people we are doing it with. We need one another. So how do we rise above gender polarization and find our way back to one another? We do it by peeling back the labels that are dividing us and leaning into the humanity that unites us. It's time we stop behaving as genders and, instead, start behaving as humans. Men are not from Mars. Women are not from Venus. We are all inhabitants of Earth. One people. One race. Humanity holds much more potential than we currently realize. Treating each other with compassion and understanding is one of the most powerful things we can do.

Humanity holds an embarrassment of riches in the personal power department. The fact of it is hidden in the word "human," if you know how to decipher it. HU is one of the oldest names for "God." Egyptian, Indian, Celtic, Tibetan, Sufi, and Native American spiritual traditions all refer to it. Take a closer look at the word "human" through that lens: Hu. Man. God and Man. To be human is to be both universal yet individual. To hold the power of both a creator and a created. It's a metaphysical oxymoron and an invitation to step into a much more powerful place from which to navigate life.

If this is the case, then the truth is we are neither spiritual beings having a human experience nor human beings having a spiritual experience. We are both. At the same time. A singular infusion of Life's energy into every single cell of our existence. In terms of a very simplistic example, it's like the color purple. Purple is composed of the colors red and blue, but if you remove either one, the color is no longer purple. Purple can only exist if red and blue are united. We are the purple in this metaphor. Instead of color, we are a seamless blend of star dust and earth dust. If we can drink this celestial and cellular cocktail, as a race we can become something entirely different than what we see and experience today.

The simple truth is that, at our core, we are all the same. Not just because we have the same color blood pumping through our veins but because we have the same powerful source energy coursing through every cell of our bodies. Our energetic origin is identical, but the label-driven operating systems we have been living with have distorted our views and obscured our ability to understand and access this sameness.

When we focus on the label, we dehumanize the person. When we dehumanize, we detach. And detachment opens the door to divisiveness. The prevailing gender norms that we've been conditioned to believe sow seeds of separation and grow division between human beings who were never meant to be divided.

The first of our labels, the gender labels we were pinned with long before we were born, have, over the course of time, led us astray. They've focused us on our differences instead of our similarities. They've justified mistreating one another, and this has led to misgivings with one another. Through the dynamics of divisiveness in traditional gender labels, the trust between men and women, as well as those who identify outside these labels, has been broken over and over. This constitutes a crisis for brand humanity.

Broken trust is something we branding experts are often called upon to repair. Losing the trust of customers qualifies as a brand crisis. The threat is immediate and long reaching. When consumers don't trust a brand, they won't engage with it, which impacts the brand's ability to hold on to business. Compounding the issue, these consumers won't advocate for the brand, either, which impacts growth. When trust is broken, all the spin in the world isn't going to fix the problem. The only way to right that relationship and step back onto a happy path is to face the music. If you want to be a grown-up, you need to own up to the behavior that did the damage and make a meaningful change. Enter the rebrand.

Rebranding is a practice through which a brand can pivot in a more positive direction. So, if brands can do it, why not people? The time has come to make meaningful change and redirect into a more positive relationship with one another, and I'm suggesting we use the fundamentals of rebranding to guide us through this shift. When done right, the practice can be as effective for human brands as it is for corporate brands. A brand is more than an identity—it's an authentic expression of self. On both professional and personal levels, a well-developed brand is a tried-and-true means of showing the world what you stand for and what you have to offer.

Properly implemented, a rebrand will stem from a brand's DNA—the crux of what the brand is all about. There is a refresh of vision and mission through which the brand promise is elevated and renewed. When done incorrectly, the shift focuses only on the brand's visual identity with things like its logo and color tweaks. If you are looking for real change, the latter is a futile exercise because a logo is just a symbol and symbols are nothing more than labels. If you've been paying any sort of attention, you know that tweaking a label isn't going to take you anywhere worth going.

CHAPTER 6

Disrupting the Label

Regardless of race, creed, color, ability, affiliation, or orientation, gender is one label we have all experienced in one way or another. Whether learning to live within or beyond its confines, this label sits at the heart of human experience. Which makes it an ideal focus for a human rebrand.

Understanding what isn't working about current positioning is the first step in any rebrand. And, as we've fairly well established, there are some fundamental things that aren't currently working between the brands "male" and "female." So, what does a brand do when it's brave enough to face the fact that change is needed? It pivots. I am talking about a minor modification, not a giant leap. Rebranding isn't meant to strip things back to the studs. That would equate to an identity crisis and just confuse people. The strategy is to subtly shift the way the brand is regarded, and in doing so, create a pivot point for moving forward in a new direction. Pinpointing the shift can take immense time and effort. But once identified, it usually looks fairly simple and seemingly insignificant.

The subtle shift of this human rebrand is to shed our traditional titles of "male" and "female" and step into a greater understanding of what it means to be "masculine" and "feminine." Sound like I'm splitting hairs? Stick with me.

I'm going to pick a little fight with the thesaurus. Whoever first decided that the words masculine and feminine were synonyms for the words male and female was asleep at the wheel. For far too long these words have been lumped into the same category, but the truth is they aren't actually synonymous and really ought not be used interchangeably. The words "male" and "female" define sex. A singular designation. The words "masculine" and "feminine," on the other hand, define energy, which is a fluid and expressive dynamic. Masculine energy does not belong only to men. And feminine energy does not belong only to women. We all embody both.

The essence of human nature, at its most fundamental, is a combination of masculine and feminine energies. Masculine energy is outwardly expressive. It's active and exertive. Feminine energy is inwardly focused. It's nurturing and receptive. While seemingly diametrically opposed, these energies are one hundred percent synergistic and reliant on each other. One is the fertile ground that allows the other to take root, and if you look closely, you'll see this interplay in basically everything. An obvious example is sexual. The penis is outward facing and expresses sperm, while the vagina is an internal vessel that receives it. From this, life is sustained. But, like I said, that is just the most obvious of examples. There are millions of examples of expressive and receptive energies working in creative collaboration.

Take the ocean for example. A wave crashes against the shore, an outward expression of the body of water—masculine energy in action. Then, the tide pulls the water back, drawing it inward—feminine energy in action. It's the opposing forces operating synergistically that make things work. Imagine what would happen if there were no feminine counterpart, and waves only crashed outward. Eventually, the ocean would run out of water and cease to be. In this example, feminine energy balances the scales and allows for sustained success; in other instances, it's the male energy.

Consider the process of innovation. In order to generate an original thought, the mind first exercises the feminine principle. It opens itself and receives the new idea. Then, within a quiet place of contemplation, that idea grows and takes form. But the feminine stillness needs the masculine thrust for that original idea to reach its potential. Without the complementary masculine energy to express the thinking, the new thought would never reach the light of day. It takes the feminine energy receiving the new idea and nurturing it into being and the masculine energy expressing it for anyone to share the original idea with the world. Only when both dynamics are in play can innovation unfold and progress be made. It bears repeating. So, I'm going to say it again: *both* of these energies interacting with one another are the only recipe for success. Collaboration is not optional—it's essential.

I hope you are starting to see the power that lies in the subtle shift in perspective from men and women to masculine and feminine. It might seem simple but with this pivot comes the ability to change the gender dynamic in bigger ways. When we rebrand our understanding of self as not just male and female but masculine and feminine, a myriad of cool things happen. First, we step into a state of organic partnership and create a unity mindset. That positions us to better understand and respect one another. Second, we expand our understanding of ourselves. When you realize that you hold both the masculine and the feminine inside yourself, you are positioned to much more powerfully evolve. You'll be able to see where you are behaving with too much of one and not enough of the other and, in turn, bring those elements into balance. If you aren't taking enough quiet time to look within, you need more feminine. If you are not putting yourself out there enough, you need more masculine. The repositioning of our mindsets allows us to take ownership of our behaviors and gives us a path forward to make needed changes. And when you change the world within, the world around you will start to change as well.

Through this rebrand, it becomes apparent that we are all MVPs meant to work with, not against, one another. Masculine and feminine energies are the yin and yang of life—totally independent yet interdependent. When you consider gender from this perspective, there can be no such thing as the greater or weaker sex. Which is excellent because it's about time we put the whole "weaker sex" myth to rest. That great human misstep came when some group of numbnuts somewhere along the line decided that qualities such as nurturing and receptive equates to frail or passive. Nothing could be further from the truth. Feminine energy is mighty. Do you know how much energy it takes to hold space for someone or something? The amount of mastery and personal power required to be still is immense. And this stillness of feminine energy is mandatory in the process of evolution.

Think about a seed that's germinating. Without the stillness of the earth to hold it, the seed would never be able to gather energy and burst into the plant it's meant to become. The same thing for a caterpillar. The metamorphosis to butterfly could never happen without the power of feminine energy to hold space for transformation to occur and a whole new form to express itself into being. Feminine energy represents our inner strength. And the simple truth is, that type of strength is incredibly powerful and much more difficult to cultivate than muscle. It's also the energy the planet has been lacking and is in such need of at this juncture in our evolution.

While it is a fact that feminine energy is powerful, truth does not always prevail. Once the misperception of feminine energy as being weak took root, it was demoted from its rightful place as an equal partner in the creative process of life. A whole new set of labels arose that reframed feminine characteristics. Being intuitive was equated with witchcraft. Being sensual was labeled as shameful. Our ability to hold space for original creation was pigeonholed to that of baby-making.

These misperceptions mushroomed into mass consciousness, pervading and underpinning all aspects of society until women, and the value of the feminine principle, were officially and permanently relegated to being the weaker sex and living in second-class citizenship. And there we have remained for millennia.

From the moment masculine and feminine energy fell out of balance, humanity began operating out of sync. The head and the heart of Life lost touch. Masculine energy represents the head—the source—of rational intelligence. Feminine energy represents the heart—the source—of emotional intelligence. Rationality, when not balanced by emotionality, tends to be cold, harsh, and unfeeling. And that is exactly what our world has become.

When we disconnected from our collective heart, we disconnected from one another. And that initial disconnect has continued to grow. With centuries of beliefs and behaviors tipping the dynamic between masculine and feminine more and more out of balance, eventually we got to where we are now—living in a world operating with all head and very little heart. You can see how this creates a fantastically fertile breeding ground for hatred and divisiveness.

As humanity began relying more on the mind and less on the heart, masculine energy began to run amok. With time, the principle of outward expression morphed into human aggression. As people and as nations, it wasn't enough to express ourselves and our wants and needs; the imbalance compelled us to force those expressions on other people and nations whether it was welcome or not. And subsequently, violence and forcefulness took the reins of human consciousness. A lot of unfortunate things have unfolded through the resulting aggressive behavior.

Wars have been waged. Lands have been stolen. Animals have gone extinct. Human beings have been bought, sold, slaughtered, and burned at the stake. The planet has been brought to the brink of destruction. And, as has become all too obvious in recent years, the potential of the many has long been cast aside in order to perpetuate the privilege of the few.

To be clear, I am not blaming our current state of affairs on men. Aggressive behavior and privilege are often blamed in a blanket fashion on the patriarchy. But today's world condition is not simply the fault of men. Masculine energy lives in all of us. Aggression is an unbalanced energy that all of us, at the very least on occasion, have exemplified. We, the team known as the human race, have collectively created and perpetuated the imbalance. It's on all of us, not just some of us.

It's time to stop pointing fingers and start pinpointing solutions. Blame is both divisive and deceptive. The simple truth is there was a point in time when we all bought into the gender label lie. Men truly believed they were somehow superior. And women truly began to live as if they were somehow inferior. The good news is that no lie can live forever. And little by little, this one has been crumbling.

THE GREATEST COMEBACK STORY EVER TOLD

Through the centuries, there have been glimmers of the feminine principle returning to its rightful place. It can be seen in the marked milestones of the fight for equality. In the mid-1800s, women obtained the right to own property. With that, they could finally stop living as someone else's property. In the early 1900s, women won the right to drive and vote. With that, they reclaimed their voice and autonomy. As important as these accomplishments were in laying the foundation of what was to come, they alone were not enough to put a dent in the imbalance that had taken root.

Despite all this progress, as recently as the early 1950s, women were still relegated to the culturally acceptable roles a male-dominated world deemed appropriate, housewife being chief among them. In school, home economics classes taught young girls to be good wives and mothers. Our education system literally taught us to set our sights on an unpaid position that would pigeonhole our potential and deny us any of the credit for our hard work.

I'm not bashing motherhood; I'm bashing the level of respect it received. While women were responsible for all the cooking, cleaning, shopping, laundry, carpooling, dog sitting, child-rearing, and countless other tasks required to maintain the home and those who lived in it, men were somehow unilaterally considered the head of the household. So here women were: Underestimated. Underpaid. Undervalued. It was a powder keg bound to blow. And by the end of the 1950s, the pill lit the wick.

Greater reproductive freedom paved the way to greater overall freedom. Women could have sex without getting knocked up. It was a game changer. There was no longer shame in having sensual and sexual natures. It was replaced with pride and empowerment. Falling in love didn't preclude pursuing careers outside the home. This was a victory for women personally and also for feminine energy as a whole. As women began to reclaim their sexuality, they began to bring the true expression of feminine energy back into the light of day.

Progress was slow, but steady, over the next several decades. The 1970s marked significant strides in bringing sexism into the light and also when women were legally protected for their right to decide what happened to their bodies. By the 1980s, the push for equality in the professional arena grew. More and more women began gaining ground in creating financial independence and being acknowledged as professional contributors. But gaining ground at work didn't change responsibilities at home.

Women were still very much expected to do the domestic heavy lifting. One of my favorite cases in point comes from a popular television commercial at the time. It featured a successful woman who could "bring home the bacon, fry it up in a pan, and never let you forget you're a man." You've got to give it to the creators of that ad. It's no easy task to acknowledge and belittle someone all in a single thirty-second jingle.

But hey, progress is progress, and the return of the feminine principle into the world has continued. If you view it through the right lens, you can see the signs of the rebalancing of feminine energy in all kinds of places.

Culturally, the rise of feminine energy can be seen in the ascent of the concept of mindfulness, which has become a popular practice in recent years.

Mindfulness, which cultivates the ability to become aware of how you are feeling and take this into account before acting, requires both masculine and feminine energy to work together. Rationality is an expression of masculine energy. Emotionality is an expression of feminine energy. When you can understand (aka rationalize) how you are feeling (aka emotion), you act from a place of awareness, which is a balanced state. You don't lash out at a situation, which is the masculine out of whack. And you don't retreat inside yourself and hide from the situation, which is the feminine out of whack. Instead, you are able to use both energies to maintain equilibrium.

The head and the heart both play a role in the process. The balance we've been talking about is exemplified through a practice that is being embraced worldwide. If you think about it, mindfulness has soared up the charts in our world. In a very short amount of time it became part of popular and corporate culture. Its principles are embraced in schools, hospitals, and prisons, and its tenets can be heard in yoga studios, doctor's offices, and on social media platforms far and wide. Mindfulness left the temple and entered the mainstream in record time. And that's because it *works*.

There's a reason mindfulness brings peace to those who practice it. Living from its place is our natural state—the energetic balance of masculine and feminine strength through which we, as human beings, were designed to operate. And rediscovering that place feels good. The body holds ancient wisdom. Its cellular memory recognizes this natural state and, just like a homecoming, finds the deepest levels of comfort in returning to it.

Nowhere is the return of the feminine principle more obvious than in the professional arena. Companies are showing more nurturing for their employees with benefits like wellness programs and personal development initiatives. Brands are now being held accountable by more balanced consumers who are collectively demanding that people and planet are prioritized and cared for right along with profit.

As a result, sustainability, human capital, and equity are now represented in the C-suite. Billions of dollars are being pumped into community care every year, fair trade and sustainable sourcing are being prioritized, and environmentally conscious practices are taking root. That businesses today are operating toward double and triple bottom lines along with being both purpose- and profit-driven exemplifies a return of the feminine principle on mass scale. It's important to recognize this because it allows you to see that there's a much bigger picture unfolding—proof that businesses are finding their heart. Our human operating system is being rebalanced and, as a result, upgraded.

For many decades people's sole career focus was on making money and getting ahead. Greed became a ruthless master. Corporate management prioritized shareholder value over human value. Their decisions resulted in toxic ingredients and fillers being pumped into food and employed unethical supply chains that left hardworking people impoverished. Bonuses dwindled for those in the trenches and ballooned for those at the top. And all manner of crimes were committed against the environment in the name of the almighty dollar. The practice of maximizing profit at the expense of people and planet is a perfect example of the energetic imbalance we've been talking about. It's financial aggression.

Under this operating system, success has been largely defined solely by the bottom line. Money is the outward facing symbol of success—and remember, outward expression stems from the masculine. In recent decades, however, a shift has occurred. While making money is still a top priority, so is operating with purpose. Quality of life, not just quantity of cash, is a consideration when choosing a career path. Finding meaning and feeling fulfilled are now professional priorities. These are the internal riches of your life's work. And the internal is the feminine. As the balance between masculine and feminine has been happening within us as people, we have been changing as a culture. This has created a ripple effect, forcing the corporate world to change as well.

It's obvious that Life is calling for a reboot and a rebalance: it can be seen in business, in the growing numbers calling for equality and justice, even in the COVID-19 pandemic. The mandated lockdowns were a giant, global inhale that brought with them an influx of feminine energy. The world was forced to sit still. And stay still. Experiencing stillness wasn't a choice. Life made it clear that feminine energy was returning to the planet whether we liked it or not.

And in an unexpected twist, many of us found that we did like it. Perhaps it took some adjustment, but as the stillness started to register, many of us embraced it: trading in the hassle of the hustle for quieter mornings without commutes; shifting from barstools with strangers to board games with loved ones; lingering over conversations instead of rushing through them. There was peace in the quiet that was forced upon us—a peace so many of us didn't even realize existed in our extremely externally focused world. We became reacquainted with a way of being we had long forgotten. A gentler one, more in tune with the rhythm of what life was meant to be, which was very different from what we have always known it to be.

Once you discover something, it's not possible to unknow it. Humanity has rediscovered how good it feels to live in balance, and we aren't going to let it slip through our grasp again. This is what the Great Resignation, the hybrid working world, and the call for the end of divisiveness is all about. Balance. Balance.

Balance. The collective human consciousness is answering Life's call to return to our natural, more balanced way of living.

While pandemics have occurred many times throughout history, COVID-19 marks a "before and after" juncture in our human evolution. There are plenty of people who don't yet realize it, but the old ways are gone. Accepting this change is not a matter of if, but when. We can fight it and deny it all we want, but sooner or later we will find that we have no choice but to let go of the old and embrace the new. Just like a baby tooth has to bleed a little and hurt a lot before it gives way to a permanent tooth, our planet is experiencing the pain of an old structure uprooting to make room for the new, more permanent way of being to take its place. The time for rebalancing and reconnecting, both within ourselves and with each other, is here. Life is going to continue to insist on the return of balance between our creative energies.

This rebalancing brings with it a reckoning. We are going to have to own the fact that the world we have created is not working. And to support us in that process, the Universe is going to ensure that we are presented with opportunities that allow us to understand the truth of who we are and how we are meant to regard and interact with one another. Rebranding to identify with our energies rather than our labels is one of those opportunities and a step in the right direction. Gender is not a birthright—it's a form of self-expression. As such, it's not designed to be just one thing. And when we embrace the masculine and feminine within each of us, we can better understand the fluidity of it. Through finding personal balance, we find societal balance.

Rather than operate as if we are independent and separate from one another, we lean into becoming interdependent and synergistic. We are *both* masculine and feminine. We carry within us traits and tendencies that draw from these energies in a way that transcends our anatomical parts. When we begin to see each other beyond the label of gender, we are given the opportunity to elevate our understanding and deepen our appreciation of what we, individually and collectively, bring to the table.

Making the most of that opportunity means accepting some hard truths. One of which is that our way of being is broken. While there still may be many who are not willing to accept it, the fact is the systems we as people, businesses, and societies have been operating under are played out. The boundaries that we have built around our gender labels carry with them centuries of misperception and stereotyping that have rooted into inherent biases we are only just starting to realize we carry. We have been brought up in a system that has normalized the limitations and bad behaviors born from these biases to the point where many men were genuinely flabbergasted when the modern women's movement came about.

So many men were left scratching their heads, either in confusion or in horror, at the realization of what the human experience had been for women. Because of the bias, they either didn't see it was wrong or didn't see it was happening at all. Labels create giant blind spots. And giant blind spots pretty much always lead to wreckage.

This is by no means just a gender thing. Normalizing the bias inherent in any label creates the same situation. Racism is another example. The horrifying truth of how many Blacks have been jailed, abused, and murdered by a broken, toxic system have genuinely shocked many whites. White people had been living safely inside the privilege of their label and had no idea how bad it was. And even when their eyes were opened, so many still didn't realize they were part of the problem. It's hard to understand that you are the cause of a system you inherited rather than created. But perpetuating a problem is not all that different than creating it, because you are the one keeping it alive.

If you allow or invest in the label rather than the human, you're part of the problem. If you don't question a system that unilaterally promotes the progress of a segment of society, be that gender, race, or any other sector, you're part of the problem. And if you prefer to stay asleep at the wheel of unawareness rather than wake up and actively become a part of the solution, then, say it with me . . . you're part of the problem.

But here's the good news. Problems exist to be solved. And that tends to happen faster and more meaningfully when we put our heads together. From a gender perspective, this means both men and women need to learn to step out of the varying degrees of defensiveness and distrust that currently exists and into a better understanding of what each brings to the table. The movements that have been unfolding are pushing us to change not only existing behavior but also the underlying conditions that have led to it.

Course correcting is not just about hiring, mentoring, and promoting women. Certainly, that is a positive and necessary step in the right direction, but the push for gender equality is about more than equal representation in places of power. It's about a way of operating in the world that rebalances the scales. For these scales to be rebalanced holistically, they need to be rebalanced individually. As always, real change starts on the inside. If you want to truly understand your human nature, you are going to have to roll up your sleeves and get to know the personal expression of masculinity and femininity within your own skin. And if you're really willing to take an honest look at that, I'll give you a hint as to what you will find: personal imbalance.

Years of living on the surface of life with no deeper conscious understanding of who we are, combined with the imbalanced ways of being that we inherited from past generations, has left us with patterns that need dismantling. We all have personal work to do in this department. And it's work worth doing. Because when we change ourselves for the better, we do our part to change our world for the better. Balancing your individual energies will bring more balance to our collective energetic.

To be human is to be both masculine *and* feminine. These energies define our essence—the core of who each of us are. A core we innately share by the nature of simply being alive. This understanding is the common ground we need in order to come together as genders, as races, as nations, as a planet. By recognizing the energetic reality of our shared human essence, we come together from a more spiritually and energetically evolved place.

This essential shift in our understanding of who we are creates a platform upon which Brand Humanity can, at long last, shed its cultural labels, which continue to deepen the division between human beings who were never meant to be divided. In doing so, we can come together in a way that is real and irrefutable. Recognition will shed more light into our world. Connection and collaboration will plant the seeds from which a sense of true team spirit can grow. Togetherness will redefine the day.

CHAPTER 7

Life Beneath the Label

As with most anything of depth, once you peel back the outermost layer, a world of discovery awaits. Welcome to that world. A place where you get to better understand what it is you are truly made of. And that something is energy.

The term "energy" is batted around these days without a great deal of understanding as to what it really means or how to apply it. People talk about energy in terms of something we feel. We'll hear things like "That place had bad energy to it," or "I just love that person's energy." Being able to sense the energy of something is super important. Both because that means you aren't living entirely in your head, and because energy doesn't lie. If something feels like bad news, it's most likely going to be bad news and you would do well to trust your senses and get yourself out of that situation.

But energy isn't just something we sense—it's who we are. There is a reason that, when our hearts stop beating, doctors jolt them with electric currents. There is a reason why biofeedback operates through electrical sensors. There is a reason why brain waves are measured in voltage. There's a reason why we call the elements that make up atoms "electrons." And that reason is because we are, on every level . . . bottom line . . . no matter how you slice it . . . energetic beings. Energy is our common ground, our common language, our common everything.

Whether chemical or electric, it's a well-known fact that humans are made of and operate through complex systems of energy. We are energetic beings in every sense of the word—physically, mentally, emotionally, and spiritually.

Neurons fire. Ions charge. Hearts beat. In so many different ways, energetic impulses determine our ability to function in the world. We accept this when it comes to biology and psychology, but to a great extent, we've overlooked how it works in sociology and anthropology. Your personality, which is rooted in the science of sociology, operates through its own energy system. The building blocks of this system aren't synapses or neurons, but, instead, are the masculine and feminine polarities we've been discussing.

Think of masculinity and femininity as the molecules of your personality. They are the base elements that create your human nature. And just like the cells that create your human body can be influenced to develop in either healthy or unhealthy ways based on your choices, so, too, can your expression of masculine and feminine energies.

Up until this point, we have been talking about these energies in their holistic form. In the absolute, masculine and feminine are polarities that form two ends of a spectrum. In between these anchors, there are millions of ways in which they come to life. They merge, ebb, and flow in individualized ways within each of us, and that combination brings forward our personal version of human nature—thus the term *person*ality—the totally unique expressions and approach to life we each operate through. The ways in which these energetics combine and express are as vast and varied as the panorama of people who populate the planet. We are all the endless shades of gray between the black and white of the polarities.

This unending combination of male and female mixing and blending is the real gender spectrum. Where each of us lives on that spectrum depends on the degree to which we have developed and embodied our unique blend of masculine and feminine energy. And the given point we find ourselves on that spectrum is never fixed or finite. Rather, it's fluid and formative. Gender expression can change and morph because people grow, expand, and embody new energy all the time. Human expression is boundless, not binary.

TRANSLATING STEREOTYPES INTO STRENGTHS

On the highest level, masculine and feminine energy are the macro expressions of Life. But each of these break down into micro expressions of human behavior. Think of it like this: if masculine and feminine energy are the molecules of personality, then these more specific human characteristics are the atoms that make up those molecules.

Through our personalities, masculine and feminine characteristics bring to bear both our strengths and our shortcomings. When our masculine and feminine characteristics are balanced, strength is created. When they are imbalanced, it creates weakness. Whether within one person or a community, imbalanced energies weaken potential and make thriving more difficult.

There are tons of books and blogs that talk about masculine and feminine energies. Often, they boil down these characteristics into well-worn stereotypes that don't really open the door to understanding. Men are rational. Women are emotional. The broad generalization in such sweeping statements barely skim the surface of the potential in these masculine and feminine personality traits. These stereotypes that have been applied to our, supposedly, gender-specific behaviors have deceived us for centuries. They have diminished our understanding of and ability to get to know ourselves and tap into the potential that is available to us as the unique individuals that we are. Which is why here, we are going to dive deeper than our gender labels allow and prove that there is more to these, supposedly, gender-specific characteristics than meets the cultural eye.

Much like any other excavation, we'll start on the surface and then dig deep to see what lies beneath. The surface is the gender stereotype's label. What lives below is a completely neutral and androgynous human quality. The stereotypical, surface-level masculine traits that rise to the top of the list are characteristics such as rational, assertive, territorial, driven, analytical, competitive, functional, and practical. The stereotypical, surface-level feminine behavioral traits most often cited are: emotional, receptive, nurturing, calm, intuitive, creative, collaborative, and purposeful. Now, let's dive down a layer and take a look at the true potential and possibilities that exist within each of these stereotypes. Each of these powerful human behaviors is more than meets the eye, and none of them belong to one gender label or the other. Let's strip each of its gender association and look at the human potential that lives within.

MASCULINE ENERGY: LET'S BREAK IT DOWN

Rational: Rationality is about objectivity. Through this dynamic, all people on the gender spectrum access the ability to gather information and organize it without the entanglement of emotion or bias. Rationality uses the brain as it was meant to be used—to observe and process. It allows you to objectively assess what's in front of you without favoring one perspective over another. Think of rationality as your inner reporter. It gathers facts and frames them into nuggets of understanding. It's data-driven thinking—observational—focusing on what is without judgment or investment. Rationality is, by its nature, detached. It doesn't take sides. It remains neutral. One of the greatest gifts of rationality is that it doesn't personalize, which is one of human nature's more popular booby traps. When you personalize something, you stop seeing it clearly because you start looking at it through the lens of how you relate to it. It's no longer simply a matter of looking at what *is*. Now, it has become what someone thinks and feels *about* what it *is*, which colors the facts. No longer is the brain just reporting and observing data. It's now processing and categorizing the emotion and judgment that has been piled on top of that data. Rationality enables you to look at something or hear what is said about it without projecting your experiences of the past, or hope for the future, on it. This is staying in the present: accepting what you are seeing or hearing in the moment can take stress off a situation. Stress-free thinking is a rarity, which makes a certain degree of rationality a lovely thing.

Assertive: Assertiveness is about using your voice. It's a means of speaking up for yourself and speaking out against those things that don't sit right with you. Assertiveness is how you share your opinions, your gifts, your insights, and yourself with the world. We all need to be willing and able to be seen and to be heard. Assertiveness enables you to create presence for yourself instead of being passed over, unnoticed, as you go through life. This characteristic is the equivalent of raising your hand in the classroom—a way of letting others know you have something to say or share. Through assertiveness, we can put ourselves out there and in doing so receive one of the most basic of human needs—acknowledgment. We all need to be recognized. We all want to be seen and heard. Being assertive is how we set off a chain reaction that, in turn, enables others to see and hear us. When a newborn cries out to be fed, that's a person asserting a need into the world. When a kid refuses to eat broccoli, that's asserting a personal preference. When a group rises up against tyranny, that's asserting a choice to be free. When someone leaves a toxic relationship, that's asserting self-respect.

Assertion is a way of communicating who you are. It's a way of saying what you need, who you love, how you want to be treated, and the mark you want to make in the world. We can't make our mark or be acknowledged for doing so if we don't put ourselves out there. The ability to express yourself, in whatever way feels right, is genuinely inalienable. Nobody has the right to take that away from you, but assertiveness has the power to give it to you.

Territorial: Territorialism is about boundaries and the ability to both define as well as defend them. It's having what it takes to take a stand. Stake your claim. Hold your ground. This dynamic facilitates your right to own your personal space and to occupy everything from a point of view to a property claim. Being territorial enables you to establish a perimeter and a space to call your own. You'll never find your safe space if you don't first define your personal space. Whether it's physical, mental, or emotional territory, you have the right to set limits. There is clarity and compassion in letting others know what your boundaries are—that you have limits and won't tolerate anyone trespassing on them.

Self-identity is a territory you create for yourself. Doing so supports your inalienable right to operate with sovereignty. You and you alone have been given the gift of living the life you have. While plenty will try, nobody has the right to determine your boundaries or how you choose to live within them. Unfortunately, personal autonomy, the ability to live according to your own values and beliefs, is something we have to defend in this world. Once you decide who you are and what you stand for, you need to protect that space. Be discerning about who you allow in. Territorialism enables you to do that. It brings with it the spirit of guardianship that protects and provides for you and others who have been welcomed into your territory.

Driven: Drive is about acceleration. Compulsion. Galvanizing internal forces and moving the needle of life forward. It's will in action. What an ignition button does for a car, drive does for a human. And, just like a car, it takes you places. By embracing this human characteristic, we are able to push toward potential and cover new ground in our lives. Drive nudges you to act today so tomorrow is what you want it to be. It pushes you toward the next version of yourself and the next chapter in your life. We are, by our deepest nature, creatures of growth. The human spirit is designed to be ever expanding, ever advancing. Tapping into personal drive is how you respond to your spirit's call. The urge to learn more. The determination to become more. The unwillingness to let anyone hold you back. These all stem from drive. Beyond the ability to push you forward, drive is a form of self-reliance. It fans the fire within and encourages you to act on your own behalf. This, in turn, creates the experience of personal achievement, which boosts self-confidence When in balance, drive creates a virtuous cycle that prompts you to roll up your sleeves to make things happen then rewards you with the feeling of pride in your work, which turns around and amps up your drive to want to do more.

Analytical: Analysis is rationality's cool cousin that takes the data reason provides and packages it into a neat conclusion. It allows you to solve problems, discover new insights, and extrapolate meaning where there may have previously been none. Through analysis we are able to question and look before leaping. This is important; in a world of spin and deep fakes, we need to poke at information and ideas to make sure they're true and worthy before acting on them. The ability to analyze enables us to participate in this kind of examination. It empowers us to draw our own conclusions. Where rationality gathers information, analysis pulls it apart. Disassembling the facts (the what) to better understand the workings (the why). Analysis is a means of extrapolating meaning from the evidence versus organizing around it.

Destructive: Destruction gets a bad rap. It's not just about ruin or annihilation. When you look at some of its synonyms, like deconstruct or dismantle, you can more easily see how the act of destruction can help you rather than hurt you. When you deconstruct something, as we are doing with labels in this book, it can reveal the inner workings of a thing and help you better understand. And when you dismantle something, it clears the way for something new to take its place. Clearing space for new growth is a critical part of life. Sometimes branches need to be destroyed in order for the tree to thrive and grow. When executed with purpose and balance, destruction makes space for creation. Acorns have to break apart for a mighty oak to grow. Sometimes things have to fall apart in order for other things to come together. Destruction is an essential player in the process of life. It's central to the laws of physics in that without it, energy can never change form. Some of the most beautiful things in the world are a result of destruction. Take, for example, the Grand Canyon. This natural wonder resulted from water relentlessly destroying rock. The Colorado River was an incredibly destructive force to the stone surrounding it, but that is exactly what paved the way for something beautiful to come into being. There's a difference between destruction as a force and destructive behavior. Destructive behavior is the misuse of destruction as a force. It's what happens when human foible enters into the equation, and the force is deployed for selfish gain. Whether self-destructive, environmentally destructive, culturally destructive, or globally destructive, this behavior is powered by an intention to harm. It's not representative of the force of destruction, but of its misuse.

Competitive: Competition is about rising to a challenge. It's facing what's in front of you and bringing your all to the moment at hand with the intention of coming out on top. Someone with a competitive nature strives for victory, and there's nothing wrong with wanting to win. This tendency sometimes gets a bad rap because, when out of balance, it can lead to cheating and being cutthroat. But in truth, competition is a positive thing. It pushes you to be your best. To keep striving, developing, and playing the game until you reach your goal. It encourages you to try harder, dig deeper, and never give up. If you get knocked down, it says stand back up. If you fail, it says try again. Competition pushes us toward greatness and compels us to be in it to win it. It enforces focus and belief in self. It cannot and will not listen to voices in the crowd rooting for you to fail. The spirit of competition, at its heart, means believing you are a player with the right to be in the game—and that you have a real shot of winning.

Functional: Functionality is about process. It enables us to perform tasks in a particular progression in order to generate a specific outcome. The line from start to finish is linear and logical. Functionality relies on systematic behavior. It means operating sequentially and with order. It's procedural: Do this, get that. Punch a keyboard, get a letter. Eat a meal, get nutrition. Take a job, get a paycheck.

Functionality is transactional in nature. There is no deeper meaning to the exchange. It orbits around usefulness and enables orchestration, bringing various and disparate cogs and wheels together to create systems and deliver outcomes. Using only efficiency as its guide, functionality determines the order in which a given set of tasks, or steps, are accomplished. It enables us to plot a path from Point A to Point B. It is the driving force behind our every to-do list. Functionality keeps us out of overwhelm and makes the impossible possible. It enables you to break down massive demands into manageable tasks. For example, when I decided to write this book, I had to first come up with an idea, then build an outline, then break down the outline into chapters and the chapters into paragraphs and the paragraphs into words. Word by word, I was able to turn a potentially daunting goal into a fathomable process. Functionality creates order and assassinates chaos. Through it, we are empowered to define the steps of success and take them, one by one, to get to wherever it is we've set our sights on.

So, there you have it. The popular stereotypes of masculine energy deconstructed to give a clear view into the common ground that lives under the label "male." Masculinity doesn't belong to men. It lives in all of us. Its attributes are characteristics that we all, as humans, possess. And because what's good for the goose is also good for the gander, we're going to do the same thing with feminine energy.

FEMININE ENERGY: LET'S BREAK IT DOWN

Emotional: Emotion enables connection. When we score a dream job, the feeling of joy and accomplishment is what makes the moment mean so much. When we fall in love, the feelings of attraction and wonder are what bond us so strongly to another. When someone dies, it's the sorrow that makes the indelible mark. Feelings are the connective tissue of life. They bring us and hold us together. They also push and keep us apart. If we feel positive toward something or someone, we do what it takes to make a connection in order to get more of whatever it is. If we feel negative about something or someone, we do what it takes to push it away. If we didn't feel, we'd be numb, zombie-like creatures, walking through life but never really living it.

Through emotion, we stop observing life and start experiencing it. Just as, physically, the heart pumps blood through the body, enabling it to function and grow, experientially, the heart pumps emotions into our relationships and endeavors allowing us to attach and bring personal meaning to our experiences. Emotion is like glue: love connects us to our tribe; fear connects us to what we are afraid of; joy connects us to our spiritual essence; passion connects us to our goals. Emotion, and the feeling it inspires, creates currents of energy that pass between us. It's through this currency that we experience the richness of life.

Receptive: Receptivity is about acceptance. It's opening your personal borders and letting the new enter. Receptivity enables you to open your mind to new ideas, your heart to new feelings, and your eyes to new possibilities. It's the ability to offer someone or something foreign a soft place to land. Whether that is a foreign citizen landing on the shores of a new land or a foreign idea landing on the outer banks of our mind, welcoming that which is unfamiliar ushers in possibility. Receptivity calls for us to soften our edges, take the padlocks off our opinions, and operate with enough humility to accept that certain outside forces just might have things to teach us and ways to enrich us. It offers the opportunity to embrace the unknown and, with it, all the potential and possibility that change can bring. We all live within the boundaries of our comfort zones—our known mental and emotional worlds. Receptivity is opening to the unknown. Making space for the new to become the known and, in doing so, expanding into new comfort zones that allow for new experiences. As a result, a ripple effect takes place that creates a more diverse world, generates inclusion, and supports evolution. All of this stems from a willingness to be open.

Nurturing: Nurturing is about encouragement. It's the instinctual ability to encourage growth and, in doing so, to coax something or someone into reaching greater potential. Whether as simple as watering a plant or as complicated as instilling hope in someone on the brink, nurturing gives what is needed in the moment in order to support development. Parents nurture the growth of their children. Teachers nurture the growth of minds. Farmers nurture the growth of their crops. Regardless of the form it takes, nurturing is an act of generosity—a willingness to give of your time, your talent, your love, your resources—to facilitate the advancement of another. The act of nurturing feeds two of our most basic human needs. If you're the one doing the nurturing, it enables you to care for another, which is an instinct born from the depth of our hearts. And if you are receiving the nurturing, you are being supported to grow, which is all the human spirit ever wants to do. Regardless of which side of the equation you are sitting on, nurturing puts you in touch with the truest aspects of self.

Calm: Calm is a form of stillness, and it brings with it emotional autonomy. Rather than being spun up into the whirlwind of other people's stories or the turmoil that surrounds them, calm enables you to keep your center. Calm doesn't let your boss or your spouse or the bonehead driving in front of you decide what kind of a mood you are in. Calm says, "It's your life; you decide for yourself." To keep your calm in today's world takes an incredible degree of awareness and fortitude. But this degree of awareness and fortitude are worth cultivating, because calm gives you power—the power to choose. Rather than being reactive, you keep your cool and make a conscious decision about who you want to be in any given situation. And when you remain in charge of how another's words or actions make you feel, it's so much easier to see when someone is trying to manipulate you or gaslight you or force you to conform. True calm is the height of emotional maturity. It is the throne of self-governing and personal sovereignty. It enables you to command your energies with grace and use the authority of your free will to choose how you want to feel and who you want to be.

Intuitive: Intuition is the ability to see and share truth. Not factual truth but actual truth. Facts change all the time. It was once a "fact" that the world was flat. It was once a "fact" that the brain couldn't grow new cells. It was once a "fact" that Pluto was a planet and that there were only four oceans. The truth that is based on what we see is always subject to change because that's perspective, and perspective shifts. But beyond seeing is knowing, like the gut feeling we have all experienced at one time or another. You meet a person and just *know* they're the one. You listen to someone talk and just *know* that they're lying. You walk into a particular situation and just *know* you have to get out of there. Intuition enables you to see past the reality that meets the eye and into the forces at play that are driving that reality. There are always energetics and intentions at play behind the scenes of the experiences we have. Intuition focuses on these driving forces by opening your inner eye and activating what is sometimes called the sixth sense. There is power in knowing the seemingly unknowable and connecting with the energies behind the curtains of life. Discerning the intentions behind words and the agendas, both good and bad, driving someone's behavior will protect you from being manipulated and position you to engage in real conversations, not just surface ones. While reason operates through the human brain, intuition operates through the higher mind. It's the built-in ability to connect not just with your higher wisdom but that of others, then tap into that wisdom and translate it into tangible information.

Creative: Creativity is about birth—the ability to bring something into this world that didn't exist before. I'm not just talking about children. I'm talking about bringing anything new and totally original into being. Maybe it's a never-before-spoken combination of words filling a blank page to create a book. Maybe it's a series of strange symbols on a screen devising code that drives new technology. Maybe it's musical notes snatched from the silence within to create a song. Through the abracadabra of imagination, new ideas are pulled from the hat of the unknown and brought into the light of day. One second before creation, something didn't exist. Then suddenly—ta-da—it does.

Creativity is an agent of change. It draws lines and connects dots that have not previously been drawn or connected. This kind of inner vision leads to outer invention and, in doing so, changes the world in both minute and massive ways. This can't happen when living within the comfort zone of the known. Creativity is a pioneer's spirit that is willing to venture into the unknown and unseen to lead the world into new territories. The creative spirit has a reckless disregard for boundaries. It boldly goes where logic fears to tread. It plows straight through the lazy acceptance of the way the world is without so much as a *pardon me* and opens the door to show the way the world could be. Doing this requires faith—an unshakable belief that something is possible. Riding on the wings of that courage, creativity takes the world beyond its own limits and opens up new experiences for us all.

Collaborative: Collaboration is about trust. It's putting your fate into the hands of the collective and hoping you will be better for it. It takes trust to depend on others. It takes fortitude to come through for others. Collaboration gives us the ability to be there for one another. It's the theory of unification in action. Through this, different people, with different abilities and different mindsets, can come together and work as one. Collaboration creates common ground. But it will ask a lot of you in return. In this world, where so much of the pervasive mindset is self-serving, collaboration asks you to step out of the "me, me, me" mindset and focus on the greater good. It asks you to relinquish control and be open to the input of others. It asks you to humble yourself and accept that you can't go it alone. And in return for doing all this, collaboration gives us the ability to achieve something together that we would never have been able to accomplish alone. It gives us a spirit of unity and a tangible understanding that everyone has value and that value, brought to the group, makes us all better. Collaboration feeds belonging. It recognizes individual value. It invites participation. It elicits pride and enables greater strides. Collaboration brings people together with the intent of staying together. And that's a formula for magic.

Purposeful: Purpose is a gateway to meaning. It ignites the drive to understand what matters to us as individuals and how we matter to the world at large. It's the need to be sure that our time here on earth has had meaning and the unspeakably gratifying feeling that comes from making a difference, even in the smallest of ways. Through purpose, you discover what truly matters to you and carve a path that enables you to accomplish those things. You put your personal values into action and build a life around them. In doing so, you live with integrity and are true to who you are, not who anyone else tells you to be. Personal purpose drives you to live on your terms, and there is no greater form of success than that. It's rocket fuel for the soul. When purpose drives your career, work will energize you rather than deplete you. Purpose compels us to dig deeper than just the "doing" of life and discover within ourselves a reason for "being" here on this planet. It is the nonnegotiable human impulse to ensure that we have made a difference in the world and lived a life worth remembering.

Now we've done for feminine characteristics what we've done for masculine ones—peeled back the layer of the label, dug deeper than the stereotypes allow, and discovered that, in truth, these characteristics are universal. They by no means belong only to women but rather live in all of us. And by leaning into them and learning how to truly leverage them, we can all become better versions of ourselves. We can make meaningful strides toward our shared human potential.

GOODBYE POLARITY. HELLO POTENTIAL.

Human potential is gender-neutral. We all embody rationality, creativity, and all the other traits to one degree or another. We are all a blend of masculinity and femininity. The characteristics we've defined are the building blocks of our human operating systems. The unique ways in which they come together define our individual personalities. And our personalities are the means through which we, person by person, relate to one another. By consciously grasping the building blocks of human behavior, we can create fundamental change. We can build better relationships, with ourselves and with others. We can build more successful careers. We can build a more equitable culture and more unified world. This more conscious understanding is the gateway to a whole new world.

CHAPTER 8

The Synergy in Our Humanity

Now that we've drilled down far enough beneath gender labels to find the neutral human characteristics that we all share, harnessing masculine and feminine energies to rebalance ourselves and our world is a matter of chemistry. Let's return to the analogy of atoms and molecules. Masculine and feminine energy are the molecules of humanity. The specific human characteristics born from these are the atoms that make up those molecules. The ways in which these various atoms combine, then, in turn, create the "cells" that form our individual behavioral patterns. And, just like human cells, their combination can go one of two ways: creating healthy systems or unhealthy systems.

When our masculine and feminine energies are balanced, they create strengths. When out of balance, they form shortcomings. Countless dysfunctional behaviors can be traced back to an imbalance of masculine and feminine energy within our individual operating systems. And those behaviors, in turn, create dysfunction in our societal systems. As humans, we are "ground zero" for the messes we have on our hands—worldwide. When our individual behavior patterns come together, they create our cultures. And our cultures collectively determine our human anthropology. So if we, each at our own individual level, take control of our behavioral patterns, we can eventually, collectively, shift the anthropology of divisiveness to the far-reaching levels of our world.

Corporate decisions are made by people. Political policy is made by people. Religious dogma is made by . . . you guessed it . . . people. If these individuals had balanced energy systems, the decisions being made would be for the good of all rather than the agendas of a few. It's not Pollyannaish. It really is true that when we start to change on an individual scale, we can, in time, cause that way of thinking to ripple outward on a local, national, and eventually, global scale.

Restoring equilibrium begins at the individual level, where human behaviors originate. The first step is recognizing the masculine and feminine imbalance that exists within the everyday dysfunctional patterns we all grapple with. To help you start to identify the imbalances, we'll look at a few examples. Let's start with a feminine characteristic: nurturing. When in balance, the ability to nurture nourishes everything from embryos to ideas. But when there's too much of it, overbearing and enabling patterns such as helicopter parenting kick in. When there is too little, abusive patterns of neglect emerge, which stunts or destroys development. If you neglect a plant, it dies. If you overwater a plant, it dies. If you withhold affection from a person, you'll eventually kill that relationship. If you smother a person, the same result is inevitable. An imbalance on either side of the nurturing ledger creates a problem.

The same is true of any masculine imbalance. Let's use territorialism as an example. When balanced, it enables people to set healthy boundaries and protect personal space. But tip the scales out of balance in either direction and dysfunction follows. When you are lacking in this, people walk all over you. When you have too much of it, you walk all over other people. Either way, somebody is getting walked on. Too much territorialism can lead to stealing, bullying, rape, and other malevolent activities running roughshod over appropriate boundaries. Too little of it leads to being taken advantage of, people-pleasing, and resentment. If you can't define a border, you can't protect a nation. If you can't respect a border, you could start a war. Once again, an imbalance in either direction is a road to no good.

These are just a few examples of how personal behavioral patterns can grow into much larger consequences, locally as well as globally. Hopefully, they sufficiently illustrate that if we all did our part to balance our own personal energy systems, we could start to lessen, and maybe even eliminate, some of the atrocities that pervade our current culture.

And here's the beautiful thing—masculine and feminine energies were designed to balance one another. Every single one of the characteristics has an equal and opposite characteristic that can be used to bring equilibrium to our behavior patterns.

MASCULINE		FEMININE
Rational	------------------	Emotional
Assertive	------------------	Receptive
Territorial	------------------	Nurturing
Driven	------------------	Calm
Analytical	------------------	Intuitive
Destructive	------------------	Creative
Competitive	------------------	Collaborative
Function	------------------	Purpose

Though the labels and resulting culture they created would have us believe these characteristics are contradictory to one another, the truth is the characteristics are actually complementary. We are, by our very natures, meant to be allies and not opposites. While the labels "male" and "female" have corralled us into separate camps, the energetics of masculine and feminine connect us into a singular, synergized team. And when you even the scales of these energetics within yourself, you become a powerful player personally and make the whole team stronger collectively.

Take a look at the behaviors in your life that hold you back. Do you jump into overreaction mode when something doesn't go your way or become cutthroat when it comes to promotions? Are you unable to apologize or admit when you're wrong? Whatever the self-sabotaging behavior is, a solution can be found by identifying the masculine and feminine energies at play and then rolling up your sleeves and getting to work to bring balance to them. Don't get me wrong—this is definitely an easier said than done situation. We humans are stubborn to a fault. And for some weird reason we tend to be loyal to our limitations—always —at the ready to justify why everything is someone else's fault and why we shouldn't have to change.

But changing is ultimately easier than hanging on to bad behavior. If the choice is to let go of bad behavior or continue to get dragged around by it, letting go will hurt less in the long run. Let's take a closer look at the complementary characteristics and see exactly how they can be used to bring balance to personal behavior patterns.

Rational and Emotional: Ah, the eternal dance between the head and the heart. It's the world's oldest balancing act and one that pretty much all of us grapple with. Rationality, the ability to approach something from a place of logic and detachment, is a valuable ability. But too much detachment can disconnect you from those around you. Emotion balances that disconnection. Our feelings bond us to one another. So, if you're too rational and only live in your head, you may come across as cold, indifferent, or aloof. Emotion takes us out of the place of rational observation and into human connection. But too much emotionality will give you a whole different set of disfunction. Being overly emotional can turn you into a clingy partner, an alarmist, or a people pleaser. A dose of rationality will tell a clinger that space is needed. It will enable an alarmist to see through the lens of fear to what's actually happening. And it can arm a people pleaser with data to help them understand that they have already given more than enough.

When you're overly emotional, you can't always see things clearly. When you're overly logical, you can't read a room. In each instance, being able to identify the characteristic that is lacking and the one that is overcompensating becomes obvious when you approach it from the energies driving the behavior.

Assertive and Receptive: Within the dance of this dynamic lives the question of how much to give and how much to take. Assertiveness enables you to give. Receptiveness enables you to receive. If you're a person who gives too much, then everything from your bank account to your life force are going to be depleted. If you're a person who takes too much, then everything from your waistline to your closet drawers are going to be bulging with crap that weighs you down. If you're shy, lean into assertiveness as a way to help you put yourself out there. If you're a person who is constantly interrupting other people, draw from the nature of receptivity and learn to relax and take in the conversation. If you've got a kid in your classroom who is always shoving their hand in the air to be the first to answer, teach them how to let others participate. If your style of management in the workplace is to give orders all the time, you might want to consider opening yourself up to hearing ideas more often. A little dose of receptiveness goes a long way in making your team feel heard.

Being overly assertive can lead to aggressive behaviors such as dominating conversations, yelling to make a point, intimidating others, and forcing your ideas down other people's throats. Being overly receptive can make you too passive, which can lead to being undervalued and passed over for promotions. It can cripple your ability to communicate your needs, which will leave you dissatisfied and resentful when the relationships in your life don't meet those needs. It will turn you into a doormat or a wallflower or someone totally forgettable. The key, again, is balance—finding the right dose of assertiveness to speak your mind and your heart and the right dose of receptiveness to make space for others to do the same.

Territorial and Nurturing: Territoriality is the ability to claim something as your own. That can be a tangible thing like a plot of land or something less tangible like an idea. It draws a line in the sand and puts the world on notice that you are claiming something as your own. Territoriality focuses on the outward border. But the other side of that coin is the inward world that is created by that border. Everything you claim—be it that plot of land or that idea—won't amount to much if you don't tend to it, which is where nurturing comes in. Think of this as the balance between house and home. Territoriality defines the perimeters of your house and imbues you with the drive to protect that space. But if you want to turn that house into a home, it needs a little nurturing. You need to care for that home, tend to it, fill it with love. It's the yin and yang that makes the magic. Territoriality creates physical space. Nurturing creates emotional space.

When territorial behavior is out of whack, it takes on many forms. You see it in people who are overly protective, super defensive, pathologically private, or emotionally guarded. When confronted with such people, a little nurturing goes a long way. By creating a dynamic or environment that feels safe, you can calm the fears of an overly protective person, help heal the wounds that create defensiveness, coax a person from the depth of their guarded state. When trust is nurtured, boundaries can be relaxed, creating an internal sense of security to match the external security of the physical perimeter.

Driven and Calm: Drive takes you places. Calm keeps you still. If you're a driven person, you will get to where you want to be in life. And if you balance that with calm, you'll be able to slow down enough to enjoy the journey as well as the destination once you reach it. Too much drive puts you in overdrive. This causes you to push too hard and expect too much of yourself, which results in anxiety and burnout. It can turn a goal into an obsession, which gives rise to cutthroat behavior and turns relentlessness into ruthlessness. Overdrive can create tunnel vision—losing sight of everyone and everything except the goal—which leads to callousness and total disregard for the feelings and needs of those around you. A dose of calm can take the pedal off the metal of drive and bring peace and perspective back into the picture. Calm allows you to pace your progress in a way that lessens angst and takes the edge off achievement. It widens the lens of tunnel vision and enables you to relax and take a little time off to recharge. Calm is a neutralizing force that can downshift drive when need be and keep you from burning out.

On the flip side, being too chill neutralizes passion. And without the fire that makes you burn for something, motivation is hard to come by. People who are too laid back run the risk of being lazy, which leads to procrastination, being a couch potato, and coming up with all sorts of excuses why it's okay to give up, or worse, not trying at all. Too much being laid back and going with the flow isn't going to lead you anywhere. Without a healthy dose of drive to balance things out, dreams and goals become unattainable. This can lead to depression, low self-esteem, and blaming others for your failures, also known as victimhood. All calm with no drive thwarts progress and undermines needed change. It leads to apathy, which leads to stagnancy, which leads to absolutely nothing. When this is the case, drive brings balance. It will ignite a fire in the belly and motivate you to make some moves. It'll infuse your sit back and relax with a little giddy up and go, giving you the kick to the backside you need to turn dispassion into passion and make magic happen in your life.

Analytical and Intuitive: Analysis is about learning. Intuition is about knowing. Once we learn the facts about something, we need to determine for ourselves if they feel true. Intuition enables us to decide for ourselves whether something is or isn't accurate. When in balance, they're the perfect combination. But if a person is overly analytical, they can become too reliant on information and get stuck on the merry-go-round of over analysis. Rather than being able to make any decisions with gut instinct, they just continually search for more information, more data, more evidence. This type of information addiction makes things more complicated than they need to be and leads to thinking things to death, continually tinkering with information and data without following the line of thought through to a solid conclusion. This kind of experimentation spin cycle keeps going around and around, making no traction, and keeps a person stewing in a tide pool of indecision or what is often called analysis paralysis. Balancing this requires finding conviction. Breaking free from these kinds of cycles requires getting out of your head and leaning into your gut. In other words, you need a little intuition nudging you in one direction or the other. Too much attention to the details can prioritize precision over progress and trap you in the tyranny of perfectionism. Here, you need to balance with a little instinct—knowing when good enough is actually good enough.

Conversely, too much intuition can leave you with your head in the clouds. It's a powerful tool to be able to sneak a peek behind the curtain of life and see a different, bigger picture. But too much of that focus may cause you to lose sight of reality. We can't completely ignore the facts as they are presented, no matter how big of a picture we can see. Intuition lives outside of conscious reasoning. It's a valid means of getting information. But without the balancing energy of analysis, taking a good, hard look at the intuitive data might lead to snap decisions. Operating only from intuition can lead to impetuousness and leaping before you look. Analysis brings balance to those behaviors by offering a dose of caution that enables you to examine potential risks before acting. Through analysis, you can slow down and determine if and when to act on the information intuition provides. People who rely too heavily on intuitive data often ignore the reality of the situation. *Feeling certain* that your ship is about to come in doesn't mean you should spend money that you don't yet have. The truth of genuine intuition is always real. But it doesn't always operate in real time, which is why its counterpart, analysis, can be such a valuable ally.

Destructive and Creative: Here is another pair of perfectly interdependent agents. Destruction removes something from existence. Creation brings something into existence. If all we did was destroy, we'd be left with nothing. If all we did was create, we'd run out of space in which to exist. Properly deployed, destruction can be a good thing. Controlled forest burns create healthier ecosystems. In destroying Web 2.0, Web 3.0 will create a way for us to be more connected as well as empower us to own our data rather than be manipulated by it. Even this book is infused with the energy of destruction: the entire premise is to offer insights that will help bring down the systems that corral us into categories of bias and feed the divisiveness that holds us apart. But my vision to destroy systematic divisiveness is balanced by a vision to create a world where we understand how to celebrate ourselves and each other. When operating in balance, destruction and creativity are a dynamic duo.

It's when destruction is driven by ill intent that it becomes imbalanced. Destructive humans want to bring things down for personal reasons: greed, insecurity, fear. When not balanced by a vision of creation, destruction is ruthless and undermining. Destructive behaviors include belittling others, negativity, self-sabotage, and malicious criticism. Destructive criticism intends to bring someone down. On the other hand, constructive criticism focuses on how to create something better. Criticism, when not powered by kindness, is an insidious form of destruction, especially when you turn it on yourself. Internal smack talk decimates self-confidence, renders you deaf to the positive reinforcement in your life, and holds you back from being the one thing you were born to be: yourself. If there is one destructive behavior that's in need of being spectacularly destroyed, it's the mean-spirited things we tell ourselves. Creativity, the ultimate form of self-expression, is the antidote to this sort of self-destruction. By its very nature, it encourages you to believe in what you have to offer and find a unique way to bring it into the world. Creativity encourages you to engage in the process of making, not judge the result of whatever that might be. It coaxes you to lean into self-trust and self-celebration.

Competitive and Collaborative: Competitiveness is the urge to win. It's one of the strongest motivational tools we have in our personal toolbox. But wanting anything too much, particularly winning, leads to problems. Glory-grabbing, bragging, and cheating are a few of the bad behaviors that spring up when competitive natures fall out of balance. In each instance, collaboration holds the power to balance dysfunctional behaviors. Glory-grabbing is taking more credit than you're due. Collaboration balances it by redistributing credit to the whole team. Bragging is a form of hoarding attention. Besides being totally obnoxious, it's incredibly selfish to continuously steal the spotlight for yourself. Collaboration, on the other hand, is generous. It freely shares the spotlight with others and makes space for everyone to shine. Cheating is the manifestation of fear of losing. It's a status thing. When a person or group is so afraid of not being seen as the best, they give themselves permission to bring out their worst. It leads to dishonorable behavior that, in all instances, negates someone else's right to win. The spirit of teamwork and a rising tide lifts all boats starts with being willing to let all boats rise.

On the other end of the spectrum, being overly collaborative comes with its own land mines. It can make you unwilling to speak up and to make decisions. How many times have you heard this conversation:

"What do you want to do?"

"I don't care. What do *you* want to do?"

"I want to do what you want to do."

With too much collaboration, nobody takes the lead. And in the absence of leadership, forward progress comes to a halt. In addition to thwarting forward motion, being overly accommodating can make it hard to say no, and often, no is the right thing to say. A healthy dose of competitive spirit can balance the scales in these instances. Group success requires some competitive spirit. It pushes us to bring our best. And bringing your best to the team is a good thing.

Function and Purpose: Functionality is the ability to deliver on a particular task. Purpose is a driving force that gives meaning as to why putting out that effort matters. Highly functional people are methodical, efficient, detail-driven, and task-oriented. When in balance, all are very valuable traits to have, but out of balance, they can result in rigidity and tunnel vision. Too much focus on process can lead to being strangled by structure. Too heavy of a focus on driving efficiency creates a quantity over quality mentality where progress is the priority and getting the job done is more important than getting it done well. And too much attention to detail creates a micromanager mentality or leaves you so preoccupied with dotting i's and crossing t's that your contribution starts to come across as inconsequential. Purpose is the antidote. It transforms the mundane into a mission that you can connect to and ties your day-to-day work to your personal values and passions, which ignites passion and motivation. Purpose makes all work essential because even the smallest of tasks plays a role in building a bigger picture. On the flip side, over indexing on purpose can put too much focus on the vision and not enough on the steps required to make it a reality. Purpose needs a plan. And functional thinking allows that plan to be put in place. Functionality lays out a path for purpose to walk on to make meaningful change in the world. Without functionality, nothing works. Without purpose, nothing matters.

The yin and yang of masculine and feminine energies represents alchemy at its finest. By blending the two together in just the right way, we can transform one type of personal behavior to another, more beneficial one. This applies both personally and professionally. Every one of the human traits we've outlined translates directly into a proven professional strength that, when balanced, can position you to excel in your career and build greater degrees of success.

TRANSLATING PERSONAL TRAITS
INTO PROFESSIONAL STRENGTHS

Okay, a quick review of our rebrand so far. First, we peeled away the labels of male and female as a way to bring to the fore the understanding of masculine and feminine energies. Then, we did a little more excavating to unearth the specific characteristics associated with each of those dynamics. From there, we dug deep into the behaviors that personify those characteristics to illustrate that they are, at their core, human behaviors that don't belong to any label but are, instead, traits that are simply a part of the human nature of us all. It was at this juncture that gender-polarizing perspectives and finger-pointing stopped. At this depth, the traits are no longer weaponized by the "us and them" mentality of girls versus boys and now paves the way for a "we" mentality placing everyone on the same team.

With this unified common ground established, we then explored the fact that these human traits, which we all possess, innately hold the power to balance each other out and, in doing so, wipe out a degree of the dysfunction and divisiveness that we operate within, as individuals and societies. Now, we know we have what it takes within us to change and heal ourselves and our world if we're willing to roll up our sleeves and do the work. But life isn't all about balancing our weaknesses. It's also about leveraging our strengths.

With all this foundation beneath our feet, let's turn our lens to look at how we can leverage our human characteristics to reach greater levels of success. Here, we will take this gender rebrand theory and turn it to practical application. This is going to be fun because all of our human characteristics have aliases—little alter egos that allow us to tap into these strengths in different ways, depending on which arena of life we find ourselves in. Let's take, for example, the business arena. Every single human characteristic we've been talking about translates directly into a proven business strength. Once you get to know these characteristics by their other names, you can more readily tap into them and ramp up or down certain tendencies and abilities in order to do better, be more impactful, and contribute more meaningfully. Let's break it down characteristic by characteristic and see how we can capitalize on who we are personally in order to excel professionally

Rational, aka Data Driven: Rational thinking is a means of gathering intelligence, and the ability to gather data is highly revered in business. Investment in the worldwide big-data market is predicted to reach more than $234 billion by 2026.[8] When companies invest their money like that in data, you can bet they are going to invest, as well, in the people who can turn that data into value. It's a critical skill in mining opportunities, determining the cause of problems, and creating strategies to help companies effectively retain talent, grow profit, and remain competitive across the board. As long as data is king, rationality will reign as a highly prized skill in the business world.

Emotional, aka Passionate: As people, emotion is what engages us. And business people, the more we are engaged, the more productive we become. Passion is the height of personal engagement. Passion means you care—deeply. And being a deeply engaged employee makes you a deeply valuable asset to both your company and your career. Disengaged employees cost the world an unbelievable $7.8 trillion in lost productivity.[9] With numbers like that on the line, if you have passion for your work, you are part of the solution to a very big problem, and there is job security in that.

Territorial, aka Protecting Market Share: Protecting market share is ground zero for long-term value creation, and this is what business is all about. In other words, territorialism sits at the heart of capitalism. And when you can tap into it to protect profit, the value of that ripples out in both financial and human ways. Protecting profit protects jobs—the livelihood of your employees. When you grow your profit, you can better invest in the development and growth of those people, which is essential to remaining competitive and avoiding attrition. Beyond the bottom line and market share, there are all kinds of productive ways in which territorialism is deployed in business. Trademarking is a form of territorialism. Cybersecurity is another. Territorial leaders protect their teams. Territorial people ensure they get credit when it's due. Territorialism is needed to keep your work-life balance in check by ensuring work doesn't trespass into needed personal and

---

8 GlobeNewswire: Big Data Market to Reach 234 Billion by 2026.
9 Gallup: State of the Global Workplace: 2022 Report.

family time. If you know how to appropriately implement your territorial nature, the value it provides can ripple far and wide.

Receptive, aka Listening: Listening is the ability to openly receive the perspectives, feelings, and gestures of others. And it's one of the greatest strategic advantages a person can have in their professional career. When you truly understand what someone needs, you can meaningfully deliver. You can also meaningfully connect, because listening is a powerful tool for connecting with others. In today's world of hybrid and remote work, feeling connected to our colleagues is more important than ever. Studies show that job satisfaction nearly doubles when employees build strong relationships at work.[10] Whether in person or on a screen, genuinely listening makes people feel that they have a voice and that what they have to say matters. This deepens engagement and builds stronger teams. An employee who feels that their voice is heard in the workplace is almost five times more likely to feel empowered to deliver their best work.[11] Feeling seen and heard is an essential human need, and if you can do that for another through listening, you have a superpower. Customers will gravitate to you. Employees will love working for you. Executives will do what it takes to keep you and foster your growth.

Assertive, aka Communicative: Assertiveness allows you to be direct and effective in your communications. That's professionally invaluable. Eighty-six percent of executives and employees cite lack of effective communication as the main cause for workplace failures.[12] However, organizations with effective communication programs are 3.5 times more likely to outperform their peers. If you can deliver information clearly and confidently, you bring something valuable to the table for your organization. More importantly, you are setting yourself up for success within that organization. When you know how to use your voice at work, your ideas will be heard, your initiative will be noticed, and your presentations will be more impactful. Good communication skills enable you to readily resolve conflict and offer the kind of transparency that instills a sense of security in the team, and this will help earn their trust. With good communication skills, you hold the power to build strong, trusting relationships that are the bedrock of good morale and loyal clientele.

---

10 National Business Research Institute: The Truth about Job Satisfaction & Friends at Work.

11 Salesforce: Understanding the Business Impact of Inclusive Leadership, Expert Markets.

12 Salesforce: The Importance of Effective Workplace Communication.

Nurturing, aka Mentorship: If you have the ability to mentor talent, you are not only an asset but you bring value to every level of your organization, including culture and investments. Culturally, 90 percent of employees who had a mentor are happy at work.[13] From a career path perspective, 86 percent of CEOs agree that mentors were a crucial part of their accomplishments.[14] And when it comes to ROI, studies show that executive coaching has a 788 percent return on investment based on factors including increases in productivity and employee retention.[15] Anyone who ever bought into the gender-slandering notion that nurturers belong in the bedroom and not the boardroom was dead wrong. Today's emerging talent is looking for mentors, not managers. They value relationships with leaders who model what's possible for their growing careers and back it up with the guidance and encouragement to help them get to where they want to go. We owe them that. And mentorship is what empowers us to give them that.

Driven, aka Motivated: The sad and well-known truth is that we have a world of workers who have no personal connection to their job. This is the definition of disengagement, and it applies to 68 percent of the workforce.[16] That amounts to a severe motivational crisis. So, if you happen to possess personal motivation in your job, you can bet you are going to stand out amid the vast majority of your colleagues who are just phoning it in. Personal motivation is the antithesis of entitlement. Instead of sitting back and waiting for someone to hand you accomplishment, you show a little gumption and seek out the challenge for yourself. Motivated people take responsibility for their lives and careers. And they do it in the most powerful way—by taking action. By proactively setting goals and taking the steps to reach them, you do something incredibly powerful— you step into leadership in your own life. And that's essential because only you were born to play that role. Being the leader in your own life is critical to personal happiness as well as professional success.

Calm, aka Composure: Composure separates leaders from managers. Because when the rubber hits the road, this level of emotional intelligence will make or break a team. In times of crisis or uncertainty, people will look to those in charge for guidance and reassurance. And when they do, they'll see one of two things: a

---

13 Nine in Ten Workers Who Have a Career Mentor Say They Are Happy in Their Jobs.
14 Vistage Research and Insights: Leadership Mentoring Matters for CEOs.
15 American University: The ROI of Executive Coaching.
16 Gallup: US Employee Engagement Slump Continues.

person they want to follow into the fire or one they want to push into the fire. Please, please, please, be the leader they want to follow, because there aren't enough of them. Studies show that 53 percent of managers get more closed-minded and controlling in times of high stress.[17] This doesn't do anybody any good. Stressed-out bosses stress out their employees. This trickle-down effect ripples through teams, departments, and organizations as a whole, negatively impacting everything from morale to productivity to talent retention. When faced with a boss who is prone to anger or unwilling to listen, employees will walk away. Composure enables you to be a mindful leader in good times and bad. It allows you to take a beat and think things through, which in turn makes for good decision-making rather than knee-jerk reactions. It empowers you to create a psychologically safe space for others. And this is not a squishy soft skill. It matters. Eighty-nine percent of people consider it essential that leaders create a safe workplace.[18] We show who we really are when under pressure. These are the moments your teammates, at every level of rank, will remember. If you can keep your cool when the chips are down, you show that you are a valuable asset to any organization.

Destructive, aka Disruptive: Disruption is the darling of the business world. Disruptive ideas are the gateway to change, and change accelerates growth and paves the way for transformation. Seventy-eight percent of executives report that they are looking to transform their companies.[19] If you can bring disruptive thinking to the job, you are an asset. You can challenge the status quo and shake up business as usual. Breakthrough thinking shapes and defines industries. It upends systems of bias within companies in those industries. And it opens doors to new, more sustainable business models that can protect our planet and all the life that lives upon it. In other words, it's good for profit, people, and planet. We need to destroy certain things in order to rebuild. Disruption allows us to do that—it is the point of change that shifts us from living in the problem to finding its solution. If you have the ability to embrace your disruptive nature, you can be the dissenting voice when needed. You can pressure-test ideas and poke holes in thinking in order to make it stronger. Negating is not always being negative. Sometimes it leads to needed change.

---

17 Harvard Business Review: When Managers Break Down under Pressure, So Do Their Teams.
18 McKinsey & Company: Is It Safe?
19 PwC Strategy&: Great Expectations: Global Executives Respond to Business Disruption.

Creative, aka Innovation: You'd have to be living under a pretty prehistoric rock not to know the value that's placed on innovation in our shared realm of industry. If you're an innovative thinker who can consistently bring smart, creative ideas to the table, solve problems in original ways, and break new ground to improve products and processes, you're going to have teams and companies fighting over who gets to have you among their ranks. Innovation is the only way around business Darwinism. Companies with "survival of the fittest" mindsets work around the ability of a brand to predict and adapt to the demands of the day. So, there's no surprise that 97 percent of CEOs worldwide see innovation as a top priority for their business.[20] With a creative mindset, you don't just survive in the face of change, you thrive in it, which explains why brands perceived as highly innovative have grown seven times faster than their competitors.[21] When you bring a creative mindset to your job, you tap into optimism and the belief that there's always a solution to whatever challenges you face. This inspires others and contagiously spreads a can-do attitude to the entire team. Creativity encourages you to try new things and take risks, which, in turn, pushes the needle forward and brings focus to new possibilities. That's a mindset anyone worth working with or for will value.

Competitive, aka Achievement oriented: The drive to achieve can make you a top performer. And being considered top talent at your company is an exceptionally good thing. When it's time for promotions, it will put you on the top of the list. When layoffs roll around, it will put you at the bottom. High-caliber employees lead to a 33 percent increase in revenue[22] and receive merit increases that are up to 170 percent higher than their peers.[23] Performance-oriented people let their actions speak to what they are capable of. They set their sights on clear, attainable goals and don't give up until they are achieved. This kind of tenacity can be contagious, which results in those around you upping their game. In the spirit of a rising tide lifts all ships, this creates a positive, upward spiral in which everyone is delivering their strongest work. This is why high-performing individuals will always be in great demand.

Collaborative, aka Team Builder: The power of a team cannot be overestimated. When you build a strong team, you create a powerful sense of belonging, and, as

---

20 Chief Executive: Innovation Is a Top Priority for Business.
21 Kantar: Why Is Innovation So Important for Brand Growth?
22 Gallup: Culture Wins by Getting the Most Out of People.
23 Society of Human Resource Managers: Reward Top Performers Even in Lean Times.

we've already established, this is an essential human need, both inside and outside the workplace. Employees who feel a strong sense of belonging demonstrate a 50 percent reduction in turnover risk, a 56 percent increase in performance, and a 75 percent decrease in employee sick days.[24] If you can infuse a sense of community into your company, you can drive success. The word unity is a part of the word community. And when we come together, we can accomplish most anything we put our minds to. United teams trust one another. Knowing that your people have your back gives you the courage to take risks and reach a little further than you might have if you were sitting on the skinny branch all by yourself. This fosters a spirit of possibility and inclusion. And it shows the real power of building a team, which comes not just from bringing people together but by bringing out their best once you've got them together.

Analytical, aka Problem Solver: The ability to problem solve is critical to professional success. Being able to problem solve means that you can handle whatever your job throws at you. That alone will go miles in helping you succeed. But that is far from the only way this skill will set you up for the win in your job. When you can solve problems, leadership qualities emerge. You can strategize, prioritize, plan, and execute in a highly effective manner. You can troubleshoot when things go wrong; you can keep a clear head in the face of the unexpected and, in doing so, shine a light on the path forward for all those around you. Problem-solving is a form of risk mitigation, and this is a doozy of a professional skill to have. Whether it's compliance risk, cyber risk, climate risk, data risk, or people risk, exposure can cost companies billions of dollars in a single second. The average cost of a single data breach alone can cost a company almost $9.5 billion.[25] But problem-solving isn't only valuable in a crisis. In everyday mode it empowers you to focus on solutions, which makes you a positive influence rather than someone who dwells on the problems, which will make you a negative influence, which is someone nobody wants on their team.

Intuitive, aka Business Instinct: In a world where data is the little darling, instinct has become the unsung hero. Particularly in the business arena where it's often dismissed as unreliable. But as we've already discussed, intuition is the result of two of your brains operating in tandem, which amounts to bringing twice the brain power to the issue at hand. When the brain in your head taps into the one in your

---

24 Harvard Business Review: The Value of Belonging at Work.
25 IBM: Cost of a Data Breach.

gut, you suddenly have access to unconscious factors that the rational mind might not consider important. This can lead to faster, more effective decision-making. And with 57 percent of executives reporting that their decision-making time is inefficient,[26] instinct can provide the answer to a very real challenge. A drawn out, ineffective decision-making process can be a kiss of death. It can cause you to miss opportunities that arise in the moment. When the rubber hits the road, execution is the only thing that can deliver results, and operating with instinct enables faster, more effective decisions that pull the trigger on execution. In addition to quicker decisions, there are times where it can lead to better decisions. A great example of this is when hiring new employees. Even if a person checks all the boxes on your job requisition and has a lights-out, amazing resume, you have to get a feel for them. And if that instinct tells you the person doesn't fit the company culture, the best decision is to defy logic and pass. Acting on instinct is a form of self-trust. And trusting yourself and your abilities is always a positive thing.

Functional, aka Operationally-driven: There's not a company in the world that's going to last very long without being able to operate efficiently. Every department and division needs help with organization and planning in order to be efficient: finance, to maximize margins; sales, to drive revenue; human resources, to be sure that the right people are in the right roles and have what they need to succeed; IT, to be sure technology is up-to-date and doesn't malfunction; manufacturing and production, to ensure quality control and efficiency in the making of products. Being inefficient wastes money and time, hurts morale, decreases quality, and opens you up to risk. All these factors create an environment in which leadership has to focus on survival instead of strategy, which means their company will continue to tread water rather than grow. Efficiency makes a company profitable in good times and resilient in bad. In a downturn, it can save jobs. In a world where 61 percent of Americans live paycheck to paycheck,[27] this matters. Saving jobs saves families. Efficient policies and procedures protect both financial and human capital.

Purpose, aka Value-Driven: Values define a culture, and a culture defines every other experience of a workplace. Everything from day-to-day happiness to year-over-year success can be traced back to the power of culture. And when that culture is value driven, positive outcomes follow. Seventy-five percent of

---

26 McKinsey: Decision Making in the Age of Urgency.
27 Lending Club: Sixty Percent of Americans are Now Living Paycheck to Paycheck.

employees expect their employers to do what's socially right.[28] Doing so makes you more competitive in recruiting talent. Furthermore, brands who put their values into action with a purpose that focuses on improving society outperform the stock market by 120 percent.[29] An organization without purpose has a task-driven culture, which is uninspiring. It drives its employees to work for a living, whereas purpose inspires them to work to make a difference. So much of our life's energy is poured into our careers. We need that time to mean something. Purpose brings that meaning. Employees who have purpose in their work are personally invested and become more than a cog in a corporate wheel—they become a driver toward making meaningful change for a better world. No job that can ignite that sort of purpose and passion, regardless of pay or skill level, could ever be menial.

THE POWER OF ENERGETIC INTELLIGENCE

Are you feeling empowered? I hope so. Because now you know that within the human nature you were born with, you have what it takes to win: drive, tenacity, reasoning, peacemaking, problem-solving, discernment, connection, creativity, protection, growth. It's all there for you—the strengths inherent in your masculine and feminine energies—just waiting beneath the outdated gender labels that have obscured their power for far too long. There are monumental levels of strength, potential, and self-empowerment that open when you get to know yourself on the energetic level.

When you know what you're capable of, you can't be pigeonholed. When you know who you are, you can't be manipulated. Most importantly, when you know you are inherently connected, you can't be isolated. With this, divisiveness melts away. Embracing the truth that we are all made up of masculine and feminine energies and all its foundations means accepting that there really is a level at which we are all equal. It just happens to exist a few clicks in from the level we currently live on. Beneath the gender labels, there is no his or hers. There is only ours.

We are all electromagnetic beings, expressing ourselves through the energy of life, all of which sits somewhere on the spectrum of the masculine and the feminine. When electromagnetic fields interact with each other, they create a force that is either positive or negative. Historically, the force we have created through our collective energies has been negative. But we can change the direction of the current and make it a positive. Peeling back gender labels shows

28 PwC: Global Workforce Hopes and Fears Survey.
29 Harvard Business Review: How Executive Teams Shape a Company's Purpose.

that these polarities are meant to be anything but polarizing. As we've seen, every energetic characteristic that defines us has an equal and opposite characteristic that creates balance. The human spectrum is complementary and designed to make us stronger, more balanced, and more whole by coming together. That's true interdependence. That's the pivot in perspective that brand humanity needs to thrive in the world to come.

Life is calling for us to bring greater balance and partnership to the energies of the world. And changing the world around us starts with changing the world within us. The more understanding we have of ourselves, the more understanding we can be toward one another. We are all on a shared journey of balancing the imbalances we have created individually, as communities, as nations, and as a single human race. That journey requires that we stop living on the surface where all we see are our differences and start living at depths that make it clear how profoundly connected we truly are.

PART 3

Diversity Deep Dive

CHAPTER 9

Diversity Is More than Skin Deep

We, as a culture, are in the infancy of creating equanimity in our world. Although the first steps are always wobbly, they are the most important. Without them, we'd never get anywhere. I'm so grateful for the journey toward recognizing diversity and building cultures of equity and inclusion in our schools, our companies, and our world. These steps have been hard won and have put us on the path toward progress. But we still have a ways to go. One of the wobbles we need to work out as we continue to walk this path is how to stop looking to labels as the baseline for defining what makes a human being diverse.

Currently, diversity is defined by categories: gender, race, ethnicity, age, ability, sexual orientation, and so on. That's okay. These are the very labels that have been used to lock us out of opportunity. So, it makes sense that these same labels be used as the keys to open those doors. But labels are labels, and as such, diversity markers will always be limiting, even when used for good purposes. Your true diversity is more than skin deep. You were born with gifts, talents, and passions that in no way rely on things like the color of your skin, where you were born, or who you choose to love. If you have a proclivity for music, you would have it regardless of your nationality. If you are quick-witted and funny, you are those things regardless of your gender. If you have a brain that understands and can calculate mathematics at Herculean levels, that brain is yours no matter what God you choose to believe in.

We are born with natural abilities. We are born with unique interests. We are driven by personal passions others don't have. We didn't ask for these things. We can't explain them. They have just, always—innately—been a part of us. No label gives them to us. No label takes them away from us. They are ours to express. And through their expression, we share with the world who we truly are. These are our true diversity markers, and they are as unique as the thumbprint on our hands. Political name-calling aside, we are all snowflakes—designed with unequivocal and intricate individuality that fell to the earth from unknown heights.

We aren't different just because of our looks, nationalities, love interests, and ability levels. We're different because of how those things have shaped our life experiences. Because we live in a world that swears by its labels, we are, for better or worse, treated in certain ways as a result of those labels. The way the world sees us is the way the world treats us. Through these experiences, self-worth is either validated or torn apart. Talents are either developed or diminished. A sense of security is either foundational, fleeting, or altogether foregone. Sometimes these individualized experiences create strengths that can help a person get ahead, but sometimes they create shortcomings that can hold a person back.

If people treat you like an outsider because you are an immigrant, you may develop an aloofness to protect you from that hurt. If people regard you as dangerous or suspicious when you walk down the street just because you are black, you may very rightly come to feel anger and resentment toward the injustice of that treatment. If a colleague makes more money than you just because you are a woman, you might start to believe you aren't of value. If the world celebrates your every little fart because you were born with beauty or into a family of social status, you may develop an overblown sense of self-entitlement that blinds you to the realities of life.

Marginalization, at even the smallest level, can instill a lifelong perspective that can hold you back. As an example, when I was a young girl, I was enrolled in self-defense classes so I could fight back should a rapist attack. Nobody told me to be afraid, but those lessons taught me that the world I lived in was a dangerous place in which I needed to be prepared to protect myself. They shaped how safe I felt in my skin and the degree to which I trusted strangers. Fast-forward to when I was a young woman in a male-dominated industry. In order to make the same salary as my male colleagues, I couldn't rely on promotions. I had to change jobs to get that pay bump to put me on par with them. This shaped how I believed I was valued. And that, in turn, shaped just about every relationship in my life. Relatively speaking, these events were minor, and yet the ripples of their impact created unhealthy patterns that took a great deal of personal work to unravel.

These little infractions have a compounding impact on how we view ourselves and the world we live in. And we have all had experiences like this. Depending on the labels we wear, the world presents itself as either full of promise or full of potential pitfalls. How human beings respond—the ways in which we grow or shrink as a result of the way the world treats us—is an important aspect of what defines us beneath our diversity labels. The unique sets of strengths, shortcomings, and perspectives that come with each person as a result of being marginalized need to be understood and supported in order to give everyone a fair shot at succeeding once they've stepped through the door of opportunity. When we find those strengths, we need to help the person grow them. When we find shortcomings, we need to help the person grow through them.

To succeed long-term, this deeper degree of culpability for the damage our labels have caused is needed to ensure diversity, equity, and inclusion. A diversity label doesn't begin to define who a human being is and all that person brings to the table. Diversity deep diving requires human development at the individual level, not the categorical level. We need to coach and offer people growth in a more personal way in order to create equitable chances to make the most of opportunities once they have been afforded.

Personal brand development can be a powerful means of celebrating diversity if we stop treating it like a buzzword and start mastering it as a meaningful celebration of individuality. There's a strange disconnect in the collective mind about the value of branding for products versus people. When we're branding a company, we take it very seriously. We hire proven professionals. We pay millions of dollars to build the brand and even more to promote and protect it. For personal brands, we don't do any of this. We just expect people to build their brand with no

real understanding of how to or even knowing what a personal brand actually is. Few things have been more bastardized and misapplied than the idea of a personal brand. Popular notion will tell you it's all about promoting yourself and making a favorable impression on those around you. That's a bit shortsighted and superficial, if we're being honest. Your personal brand isn't about what other people think. It's about what *you* think and how *you* feel. It's a means through which your deeper diversity can be expressed in your life. It's an opportunity to celebrate your individuality and formalize your commitment to being true to who you are.

This has to happen if you are to have any shot of experiencing authentic success. Your talents will wither if you don't use them. Your little quirks will go unloved if you hide them. Your core values will eat you alive if you betray them. When you bring these essential elements of who you innately are forward into a personal brand, you do more than express yourself—you learn to respect yourself and take a stand that tells the world to do the same. When you create a brand that expresses who you are, you pave the way for the world to see and accept you on the deepest human level. If people don't accept you, then walk away—and don't stop walking until you find the tribe that will value you for who you are.

When you choose to stand for something, the simple truth is, not everyone will respond positively. Plenty of people, customers, and potential life partners will be put off by what you stand for. No brand or person can please everyone. A well-built brand is a paradox. It both draws people to us and pushes people away from us. For those who resonate with your brand, it will create common ground. For those who don't, it will create an opportunity for tolerance and acceptance of something they don't relate to. This leans into inclusion. And we all have the right to experience it.

So how do we advance the current notion of personal branding from the surface level? The same way companies do. There are six key building blocks, and every successful and beloved brand, from global enterprises to startups, has been developed through them. These fundamentals drive stratospheric success for basic parody products every single day. Imagine what they can do for genuinely unique individuals.

The first building block is to define your unique selling proposition, also known as a USP. This is about pinpointing what makes you unique. And yes, you are unique. Each one of us brings something all our own to the table of life. This is the very definition of diversity. The USP is your competitive advantage. Once you know what your special sauce is, you will be able to find all kinds of ways to apply it in your life. Embracing and embodying genuine one-of-a-kindness is the real nugget of gold in any successful enterprise.

If you don't know what makes you unique, it's time to get to know yourself a little better. What makes you unique isn't just one thing. It's a cocktail of things blended together that create a one-of-a kind refreshing human. Defining your USP is taking those things and pulling them into a single lens of understanding.

When thinking about the unique value you bring to the table of life, don't just look at what you can do—look more deeply at *how* you do those things. Beyond skills, how you personally tackle any given situation plays a key role in identifying what it is that makes you genuinely unique. As an example, let's look at a typical work situation. You're sitting at your desk, doing your thing, when out of the blue a client reaches out with an emergency. It's an all-hands-on-deck, time-is-of-the-essence type situation. Of course, every person on the team is going to bring the skills they were hired for. But within that dynamic, generally, there's the person who brings the calm and clarity to keep things moving smoothly. There's the person who brings humor to add a little levity to the stress. And there's the person who brings the cupcakes to help everyone power through. (Thank God for the person who always brings the cupcakes.) All are examples of the unique way different people approach the same situation. And, for each of these people, that personal approach, whatever it may be, is a part of their unique proposition.

Think of your USP in terms of a bedside manner. All doctors, general practitioners, or those with specialties are required to learn the same things. Their diplomas are not what makes them stand apart. We don't choose our doctors simply because they graduated from medical school. That's table stakes. It's how a particular doctor approaches health issues and shows their humanity that draws certain people to them. This is a unique selling proposition in action. Medical diplomas grant them the label of doctor. But individuality makes them unique within that label.

Defining your brand purpose is the second block of brand building. If USP is *what* you can offer, then brand purpose is *why* you are offering it. Purpose means having a mission. And that mission revolves around the values that drive you and the change you want to see and be in the world. Purpose is the passion-driven, motivating force that makes getting out of bed everyday a worthwhile adventure. It ensures all the life energy we pour into each and every day of living is an investment in something that matters to us. And that something is always about more than making money.

As far as motivation goes, money is generic. Every brand, personal and professional, needs to make money to survive. Purpose, on the other hand, is unique and specific. Core values and personal passion are an essential part of human diversity. We all hold different things dear in our hearts. We all want to make a mark that we will be remembered for. In taking this step of personal brand building, you get really clear about what that is. And in doing so, you evolve your brand—and your life—from focusing on just money to focusing on both money and personal meaning.

When you've managed to create a personal purpose that has deep, undeniable, passion-driven meaning, you've tapped into your core. And the core is abiding. What it stands for is enduring. A brand's purpose doesn't change. How purpose is expressed may come to life in a kaleidoscope of ways, but regardless of the venue of expression, the essence remains intact. For example, let's say your purpose is to promote social justice. You can do that by being an activist who leads marches, by being a musician sharing socially just messages through song, by being a lawyer who fights for justice in the legal system, by running a company that provides equal opportunity, or by being an actor who brings stories of social justice to life on screen, thus spreading awareness. You could, if you really wanted, do all these things in a single lifetime. Doing so would be jumping all over the map, career-wise, but you would never be off-brand. As diverse as they all are, with each and every iteration, you would be doing your part, through your purpose, to forward and foster social justice in the world.

Personal meaning and passion will always carry a value that cannot be measured in dollars. You can't put a price tag on living a life that holds meaning. This is something so many people are searching for in their lives. We all deserve, and have what it takes, to share ourselves in a meaningful way. But such meaning can be very hard to find in the superficiality of labels. Which, in turn, makes it hard to find in a world that perpetuates that type of culture. The search for meaning in the world around you stems from not taking the time to define it within yourself, which is exactly what this brand building block enables you to do.

The third building block is to develop your message. Once blocks one and two are in place—identifying your unique proposition and personal purpose, the next step in your personal branding journey is to learn how to express these things in words to the world around you. In the professional arena, this is called creating compelling messaging. In the arena of personal branding, it's called finding your voice.

Your voice is a priceless gift. As is often the case with things that are simply handed to us, we tend to take our voices for granted. The ability to speak empowers us to connect with one another. This is a must-have if we want to dismantle the divisiveness that has separated us into ideological islands in our current way of living. Finding your voice and learning to speak from it is the greatest gift you can give yourself. And the world.

Here you have to learn how to let people know what you're all about— who you really are beyond your labels and how you hope to make a valuable contribution through that uniqueness. When you know how to succinctly share who you are and what you have to offer, your brand purpose converts to brand promise. You are giving your word, both literally and figuratively. Literally, you are putting into words who and what you are all about. Figuratively, these words represent your promise to the world of how you plan to be a part of this life and impactfully contribute to it.

Insecurities flare at the idea of crystallizing a personal message. We live in a critical world, and it takes bravery to put your message and your story out there. But it's bravery worth mustering. By learning to own your voice and share your message, you give your true self a stage for the world to see. Will there be critics? Sure. There always are. But there will be fans as well. The trick is to focus on your fans. Far too many people on this planet feel they are nothing special. They buy into the misguided notion that because they don't walk red carpets or make it onto the nightly news, their stories are not worth telling. Nothing could be further from the truth. There's no such thing as an ordinary person. Life is an extraordinary experience, which makes us all extraordinary simply by being a part of the grand adventure.

The next step in building a meaningful personal brand is developing the brand's image. Far too often people believe this begins and ends with creating a signature look. We live in a culture that places an inordinate amount of attention and importance on physical appearance. So, yes, this is a part of it. But what a brand looks like is *identity*, and that is not the same thing as *image*. Your brand image is much more.

Unlike looks, which are handed to individuals via genetics and handed to businesses via graphic designers, image isn't handed to us. Image is created by us. It's a reflection of how well you embody your values and live your purpose. If identity is style, then image is substance. How you act strikes an emotional chord that creates connection in a far deeper way than your looks ever could. Your behavior paints a picture of personal character. And when it comes to showing your true colors, character (image) always trumps characteristics (identity).

Your image is a living reflection of what you stand for. Defining your message empowers you to talk about who you are. Building your image is about walking that talk and learning to live your purpose, which speaks volumes to the world in a way words never can.

The fifth block in building a brand is marketing. At this point in the brand building process, you have developed everything you need to start putting yourself out there. You've done the internal work and have identified what you have to offer and aligned it with your values and passions to ensure there is meaning and personal fulfillment. You've figured out how to put this into words that allow you to talk about your value confidently, and you've determined how you can live your brand to make sure your outward reflection is aligned to the inner foundation you've created. With marketing, the rubber hits the road.

People tend to hold back when it comes to marketing themselves. There is hesitation and worry that they will come across pushy or smarmy. But done correctly, marketing is neither of those things. Marketing is a way of saying, "I'm here. And I'm willing." It's not about pushing yourself on others but about putting yourself out there. The trick is to flip the script of your mindset. Stop thinking about marketing as selling and start thinking about it as sharing. Focus on how to be of service.

Giving of your time and talent is a form of generosity. Conversely, holding back what you have to offer because you feel shy or awkward is a form of selfishness. We are meant to share who we are, and in marketing our personal brand, we learn how to do that in a way that feels easy and authentic. When you market yourself, through a resume, on LinkedIn, a dating app, a social networking conversation, or any other way, you lay the ground for common ground. It's on that commonality, where you have something to give that another person or organization wants, that connection for the betterment of everyone takes place.

It's essential to feel good about the commerce aspect of marketing yourself. There is nothing wrong with being compensated for making your contribution. Getting paid is a way for the world to recognize the value of your contributions. Be it making a sale, securing an investor, or landing a client or a job, marketing is meant to help you as much as other people. Allow the good you put into the world to come back to you. It can be a virtuous cycle. The more you receive, the more you'll have to share the next time around.

The final step in this merry little process is management. This is the never-ending step that ensures all the work up to this point pays off. Because what's the point of building a killer personal brand if you are just going to run it into the ground? There's a lot that goes into successfully running a brand, but none of it is more important than budgeting your assets. And by this, I don't just mean money. While essential to living a secure and happy life, money is not the most valuable asset a brand can have. In fact, it ranks last in the top five.

As human beings, our most valuable resources are our health, time, energy, and each other. Without them, the money is going to be a lot harder to come by. Without health—physical, mental, and emotional well-being—not only would you have a harder time performing a job but you would also be spending a great deal of money on doctors and therapists. Without time, we wouldn't be able to show up to make or spend money. Without enough energy, we would most likely be outperformed and put ourselves in a position to lose our client base or source of income. And without each other, all the money in the world would mean nothing. Money, just like the rest of us, needs other resources in order to grow and thrive.

As a leader of the venture known as you, it is your number one job to manage all your assets with as much care and attention as you do your finances. Life is so precious, and the time we have with the people in our lives simply does not last forever. As you continually grow and strive for greater levels of success, managing your assets in such a way that keeps this in perspective is what will always bring you the richest life in the long run.

That's it in a nutshell. Those are the six building blocks of a brand, loosely translated from product development into human development. Taking the time to work them will open the door to the deeper levels of your personal diversity— the key things that define your individuality in a way labels never can. These six steps will empower you to share yourself and your truths. Meaningful personal brand building is a journey into self: the deep-seated passions and values that you innately hold true; the one-of-a-kind path you've walked to get where you currently are in life; and the perspectives and insights that journey has afforded you. These things define your individuality. And your individuality is your birthright. You have the divine right to be the human you were born to be.

CHAPTER 10

The Essentials of Individuality

Let's start with a simple question: Who are you? Before you answer, here's the catch: No labels allowed. You cannot use your name, your professional title, your age, or your familial designation as a parent, child, aunt, uncle, niece, nephew, etc. You can't use your gender, nationality, ethnicity, race, sexuality, or ability status. No religious, political, cultural, or organizational affiliations are allowed. No class or demographic designations, no school mascots, no addictions or diseases. No labels of any kind. Not even the label "human being."

I'm asking you to tell me who you are without relying on the go-to answers that you already know. Not such a simple question anymore, is it? That's because the truth is most of us don't really know ourselves beyond the labels we wear. We have built our lives around our identities rather than our individuality and learned the vast majority of what we know about ourselves through indoctrination rather than exploration. In other words, our labels have limited our experience of ourselves and of one another. The belief systems we are born into sweep us up and carry us along through the early years of our lives. Then, the next thing we know, we have bills and jobs and families, and we can't find the time to go any deeper into understanding and becoming who we truly are. By the time we realize there might be more to life, we've become so entrenched in our labels and systems that we can't slow down the ride.

There is no personal shame in this. It's been the way of things for a long time. But life is changing. We've all felt the deeper stirring for more: more meaning, more purpose, more fulfillment, more connection. All of this is real. All of this is possible. And all of this revolves around accepting that what will ultimately allow for more of all those things, is discovering more in one single thing: yourself.

Step one is to humble yourself enough to admit you might not actually know yourself as well as you think you do. You are vast. You have lived lifetimes. There are worlds of experience and insight in your spiritual evolution. Every time you've taken on a human lifetime, you've continued to learn, to further develop talents, to deepen connection to specific values and love for certain activities and certain people.

All these experiences and the richness of understanding and expanded consciousness they provide don't just vaporize when you die. The body you live in decomposes, but the experiences your spirit has acquired while in that body never do. Only the human brain stops working. The spiritual mind, your consciousness, never ceases. All the memories, insights, and experiences you have had remain well and intact. People who have had past life memories, or intuitive practitioners who are able to access past lives and speak with loved ones who have passed, are connecting to this energetic library.

Each time you embody, you get to pull from this storehouse of spiritual experience and infuse some of the strengths, passions, fears, relationships, and blind spots you have had in the past into the person you are choosing to be. The choices of what to infuse into your individuality is deeply strategic. You bring the talents that can most help you succeed, the relationships that can most help you grow, the circumstances that can most help you expand your understanding of truth, and the strengths that can most help you overcome those weaknesses still in need of remedying. The decisions as to which of these things to include are not made by some distant being on high. They are made by you. Not the human you but the spiritual you. That aspect of self that lives on and sees your biggest picture is always guiding you to greater degrees of growth.

In other words, there is nothing random about the talents, traits, values, and proclivities you possess. They are all very carefully chosen by a part of you that is wiser and imbued with far more vision and insight than your human brain. These elements of your individuality have been selected by your higher wisdom to help you live the most amazing, authentic, and fulfilling life that you can. It's weird to think about making these choices for yourself and not having a conscious memory of it. That's part of the game. Through the life you live, you're meant to develop a strong and direct connection to this aspect of yourself so that you can access this wisdom consciously.

The trick to building this connection is to sit down and shut up. By sitting down, I mean meditating. Every day. At the same time and in the same spot. Learning to quiet your mind and body on a regular, rhythmic basis is the only way to tune into the silence where higher vibrations exist. By shut up, I mean once you find that silence, learn to listen. Silence every voice in your head and start to discern the voices in your head from the quiet speaking wisdom that abides in your high heart.

If you can tame your brain to the point where it stops overriding your spiritual mind with human logic, a very wise part of you will start talking. This quiet voice doesn't require a priest, deacon, or monk to stand as its translator. No dogma, creed, or sacrament is needed for you to connect. The relationship between you and Life's higher wisdom is designed to be monogamous, sacredly kept between just the two of you. This means, in addition to the chatterbox voices in your head, you'll also need to tune out any beliefs, teachings, or doctrine that has convinced you that you need an outside go-between in order to connect to higher wisdom. You don't—it's inside you. There isn't a planet in the galaxy where it makes sense to set up a toll booth inside your own heart, where someone else holds the power to let you pass onto the higher roads of spiritual insight.

Life's higher wisdom is not living out in space somewhere. It's not apart from you—it's a part of you. The term "higher self" includes the word "self" for a reason. There is a very powerful version of you waiting within. Discovering it and collaborating with it requires the discipline to journey out of the logical mind and into the silence that will take you to its doorstep.

Silence is the path that connects to the part of you that architected the elements of your individuality, but you don't need to log years on a meditation pillow to pinpoint what those elements are. That part is simple. There are four essential elements that define your individuality:

» Innate talents

» Distinguishing traits

» Developed skills

» Core values

These simple, everyday words are so much more than just words. They are the seeds of deeper diversity. And when you water and feed them with your time and energy, you will discover the essence of who you are—not as a generic soul, but as the unique, one-of-a-kind spirit who has blazed a unique, one-of-a-kind trail through the Universe.

We are all born with a diverse blend of talents, traits, passions, and values. This is the spiritual software that comes pre-wired into the hardware of our bodies. Your talents, traits, and values come into this world with you. And they would be born with you no matter what country, race, gender, sexuality, or abilities you have. If you were born with an innate gift of athleticism or are artistic, that's a part of who you are. You could strip away everything else—every label and diversity marker you can claim—and that talent would still be there. That's an innate ability. A possibility that was born the moment you were.

Some may belittle your gifts. They may reject your personality and trample all your values. But no one can take these things from you. Your core elements of individuality will live for as long as you do. These seemingly simple and ordinary things—talents, traits, values—are the love children of your spirituality and your humanity coming together. Being the person who embodies and utilizes these things, regardless of how, is your path. And it has been blessed and sanctioned by the Universe to the highest degree.

Generally speaking, as a human race we've gotten a few things wrong—one being that our spiritual paths are about where we are headed. Our sacred paths orbit around who we are. Searching externally for your true path is the equivalent of knights scouring the planet for the holy grail. You, my friend, are the holy grail. Accepting and connecting to who you really are and giving of yourself through your individualized gifts, in ways big and small, is your spiritual path to walk. It's that simple and that complicated all at the same time.

Because it might sound strange, but a lot of people can't readily rattle off what their talents, traits, skills, and values are. You'd think we'd all know such things, but the fact is, we don't currently live in a world that supports taking the time required to deeply get to know ourselves. We're encouraged to live within the labels rather than look beyond them, and as a result, we only have a vague notion or a partial understanding of just how much the individuality that lives beneath those labels truly has to offer. But here's the good news: figuring it out isn't rocket science. The process is the same one you deploy any other time you aren't sure about something. Start asking questions.

QUESTION 1: WHAT AM I GOOD AT?

The answer to this question will uncover your innate talents. These are not things you learned in school or through any sort of training. These are those things, both big and small, that you've just always naturally been able to do well, without anyone teaching you how. These natural aptitudes that you were born with can be mental, emotional, or physical in nature. Whatever they are, without much effort, you've easily excelled at them in a way that others around you most likely don't.

The natural talents you bring to the world are the ones your spiritual wisdom believed would most serve you in living a life where happiness and success could come naturally. And remember, success doesn't mean stardom. Your innate talent doesn't have to be at the level of the paintings in the Sistine Chapel. We're not talking about being a master at something or putting it on a world stage. We're talking about being good at something, and that something can be anything: big or small. It can be gardening, speaking a foreign language, training puppies, solving puzzles, being quick-witted, or having a great sense of direction.

Overlooking our strengths or passing them off as nothing special is easy to do. Our strengths come so easily to us that we might assume they come easy to everyone. Also, we tend to look at ourselves through a critical lens of never being good enough, and in doing so, we belittle our strengths. What others might see as amazing, we miss entirely. Or there's always the chance that you decided long ago that your strengths weren't worthy enough or wouldn't lead you to success, so you cast them aside and forgot about them to the point that they are now what we popularly call hidden talents.

As you sit to pinpoint your core personal strengths and innate talents, it's important to remember that they aren't always big, showstopping things. Not everybody who is great at tennis is going to become a Wimbledon champion. Talent doesn't have to be prodigy level to be authentic. It just has to be yours. And once you find it, you don't have to take it on a world stage to succeed. You just have to tap into it in the ways that work for you.

Innate gifts are a true-blue North Star pointing you in the direction your life is meant to go. It's plain common sense to lead with your strengths in all things, be it your career or your life. So, whatever it is you excel at, choose a path that enables you to use those talents. There are millions of different things you can do with your life, which can make choosing a daunting task. But when you use your innate talents as a filter, it narrows the list significantly.

Your innate talents are also points of connection to your own spiritual guidance. When you trust your gifts, you are trusting the inner wisdom that chose to infuse those gifts into your life's plan. And that's no small thing. It is, in fact, the beginning of autonomy—steering your life from your own center of truth rather than allowing the world to influence you in one direction or another.

Maybe most fun of all, your innate abilities are the world's greatest dispensers of self-validation. Tapping into your spiritual guidance puts you in touch with the part of yourself that knows you are enough, which brings validation from the inside out. And doing the things you are naturally good at will yield positive performance, bringing validation from the outside in. It's a double dose of personal endorsement. And it will make you feel powerful. Special. Invincible. Your abilities are your version of leaping over a tall building in a single bound. When you are mining your gifts and operating through them, it's impossible to feel imposter syndrome because you know, in your bones, that the successes that come your way are a result of who you are.

Where your innate gifts lead you is not nearly as important as how they will make you feel. Regardless of whether you find yourself in the corner office, behind a cash register, testing soil in the middle of a national forest, hopping along a balance beam, or at a kitchen island chopping vegetables, if you have found the feeling of certainty and self-satisfaction that comes from deploying your natural talents, you have found your place in this world.

QUESTION 2: WHAT'S MY WEIRD?

This question will help open the door to pinpointing your distinguishing traits. It empowers you to embrace all the things our culture might compel you to squash in order to fit in. In other words, it helps you embrace your one-of-a-kind personality—that mixed bag of goofy idiosyncrasies that define you and come to life in ordinary, everyday ways. This includes your demeanor, like being quiet or outgoing. It includes your weird little quirks, like snorting when you laugh or dancing when you brush your teeth. It also includes those little things you inexplicably love, like old black-and-white movies or animals; and, not to be left out of the mix, those things you inexplicably fear, like spiders or heights or clowns.

Accepting, and more importantly, openly expressing your weird little ways, is both your privilege and your right. It's your privilege because you've been given the chance to be here, on this planet, at this crazy point in time. To live in an age of reinvention, when mindsets are shifting and the rock-solid ways of the past are crumbling to make space for a more accepting, more equitable world to take hold. It's easier to be yourself today than it was a decade ago.

It's your right because you, as an autonomous spark of Universal light, have a literal divine right to express yourself freely, authentically, and without reservation. Every last little attribute that defines you is part of an intricate plan that you created. Nobody else gets to override or undermine that intelligence.

When I was a kid, I'd often go crying to my mom when someone called me weird. She always had the same answer: "Oh, honey, there's no use being weird if you can't show it." It used to drive me up tree after tree. I found no consolation in those words. But that changed. As I got older and started to understand and accept my odd little weirdo ways a bit more, I realized there was serious wisdom in what she was saying.

She didn't tell me to fit in or to accept myself. My mom actually told me to take it a step further and flaunt myself. Decades ago, she, in her own way, was giving me permission to fly my freak flag. To just go right ahead and show the world exactly who I was. That little Midwestern housewife was on to something. The woman was much wiser than the labels she wore might lead you to believe.

Your personality helps to curate your life. It will draw the people to you who will love and celebrate your individuality, surrounding you with tribe and support. Conversely, there are times when life brings people into your orbit who challenge that individuality, and this will serve you as well because it will force you to stand up for yourself, draw boundaries, and defend your uniqueness. It will also shine a light on potential areas in which you might have a little growing and changing to do.

A critical part of knowing and accepting who we are is understanding that there are things about ourselves that we may need to change. The truth is, not every trait we are born with is a healthy one. Our personality software does come with bugs. Some of our unique traits might actually be flaws that are holding us back. We have to be willing to face and fix those innate shortcomings that may be limiting us.

Generally speaking, personal flaws are characteristics that have tipped out of balance. For example, let's say you are naturally shy. That's okay. There is nothing wrong with being reserved. But if your shyness is so dominant that you allow others to treat you like a doormat or opportunities to pass you by, then your shyness is operating to your detriment. It's an example of a personality trait gone wild, and you will need to rein it in and bring balance. This is part of being human. There's nothing shameful in not being perfect. Imperfection is one of the few things we all have in common.

QUESTION 3: WHAT'S IN MY TOOLBOX?

This question helps to pinpoint your developed skills. These are your tools. The acumen, know-how, and accomplishments you have picked up through life's experiences, both personal and professional. Whereas talent is given, skill is earned. These things aren't born in you or given to you. These are the abilities you work for. A skill is less innate and more learned.

The personal tools you have acquired enable you to build your career, your relationships, and your life. They can be self-taught or learned through formalized education and training, and through professional mentoring. Regardless of how you develop them, the trick is to hone the skills that will enable you to express your talents into the world.

Your innate gifts give you the power and potential to excel at something. But it's in developing skills that you turn that potential into reality and learn how to put your talents to use. Using myself as an example, I was born with the ability to write. That is my innate talent. Throughout my life, I've built a series of different skill sets, all of which are rooted in that ability. I've learned to be a journalist, a copywriter, a screenwriter, and an author. Each required that I learn to be proficient in different processes, software, presentation skills, networking skills, and industry expectations. But in the center of every one of those skill sets sits the truth that I was born to be a writer. The innate ability is always there. Each different skill set offers a way to apply it to specific industries and share it with the world.

Your individualized toolbox includes both hard and soft skills, which correlate directly to masculine and feminine energies. Hard skills are specific and practical means through which we contribute to an end goal. They are practical and focus outward on doing something. Writing code. Analyzing data. Wiring a building for electricity. Soft skills reflect the person you are *being* while working or moving through life. Actively listening. Managing conflict. Motivating others. Your hard skills are your outward strengths. Your soft skills are your inner strength.

Hard skills are marketable, and through them you can rise to the ranks to become a manager. But only soft skills will transform you into a leader. The ability to listen, nurture talent, maturely and productively handle conflict and stress, the ability to motivate, connect, and inspire—these are leadership qualities. These are the soft skills that grow trust and loyalty. Without a strong set of soft skills, you can't build great relationships. And healthy relationships are the name of the game in both personal and professional endeavors. So, just like feminine energy, the skills may be deemed soft in title, but they are incredibly powerful in reality.

QUESTION 4:
WHAT SWORDS AM I WILLING TO FALL ON?

Here, you uncover your core values—the ideals you hold so deeply and strongly that nothing and no one gets to tread upon them. Your core values are your deepest-held convictions. The nonnegotiable personal truths that you will defend and abide by, come what may.

Your values define your character. They form your individualized code of ethics that determines your sense of right and wrong and what is and isn't okay in terms of how you live your life. They're the guiding force behind who you befriend, marry, go into business with, vote for, work for, pray to, and donate to. Values can inform how you eat, where you live, and a million other things right down to how you treat pets and whether or not you recycle. They will drive so many important decisions in your life, which is why it's essential that you make sure the values you hold are actually your own.

Values, like labels, are often inherited. For example, as infants, many of us are baptized, circumcised or, through other rituals, brought into beliefs and faiths that we know nothing about and did not consciously choose. Promises are made on our behalf that we are then expected to abide by all the days of our lives. These decisions to hold certain values and beliefs are made without our permission or consultation. They are made before we have the tools to explore who we really are, and as a result, can lead us down inauthentic paths and away from our truest individual values. This is not just a story about religion, however. It plays out with family values, political values, and cultural values as well.

We are born into a world that has very clear and well-defined camps of values. These camps are big and well-established and hold insane amounts of power to sway us. Whether purposeful or not, these ideological camps, and the dogmas and mindsets that run them, are among the most divisive in existence. If you are born Jewish, you are taught to believe you are chosen and others are not. That spells out a very clear us and them. If you are born Catholic, you are taught to believe that you have been saved while others have not. Again, us and them. If you are born Conservative, you are taught to believe that those who have abortions are grave sinners. Us and Them. If you are born Liberal, you are taught to believe that those who don't support social programs are greedy and uncaring. Us. Them. The list goes on and on.

The value camps of the world are pitting us against one another. They carry the mentality that either you are with us or against us. Either you belong or you don't. And if you don't, ostracism and isolation in the form of being disowned or excommunicated are very real possibilities. How are you ever supposed to feel free or safe determining your own values when so much is riding on accepting the ones that have been heaped upon you?

To move into a world that is more united and accepting of everyone, we are going to have to find a way to hold our values without holding them against one another. When it comes to values, it's time to step out of our camps and into our own personal truth.

It's understandable that we have adopted the values of our families, our religions, our political parties, and our companies, because, for the most part, they're positive in nature. Love. Trust. Freedom. Loyalty. Who wouldn't want to embrace that? But there are hundreds of other values that are equally as great. Humility. Kindness. Acceptance. Perhaps these values aren't glitzy and popular, but they're just as positive and potentially meaningful. And maybe some of these quieter values are the ones that feel most meaningful to you and belong in your inner circle. You have the right to explore your heart and decide for yourself what matters most to you. Values are about individuality, not group mentality.

This is not to say that belonging to groups that share your values is a bad thing. Having aligned values can be an intense bonding agent. Strong communities can be built around that sort of common ground. Shared beliefs are not the issue. The "better-than-thou" mindset of believing that one set of values is better than another is the issue. That sort of mindset is organized bigotry, and it's not doing any of us any good.

Personal core values are meant to be just that—personal. They aren't one-size-fits-all, and they are not weapons of judgment to be used in deciding who's better or holier or more in the right. They are meant to be your personal guideposts and nobody else's business. Unless you hold elitism or arrogance as your deepest conviction, you should be able to find room within yourself to live and let live in the values department.

This is not to say you need to be an island. Autonomy does not mean being alone; it means making your own decisions and being your own biggest influencer. Taking the time to get ruthlessly real with yourself and reexamining your values with an eye on discovering if any of them are just cultural values masquerading as your own is a means of reclaiming some of your personal power. It's a chance to step into stronger leadership in your own life.

FOUR QUESTIONS. ONE ANSWER.

This chapter opened by asking one simple question: Who are you? And after exploring the four sub-questions that followed, I hope you are starting to get a clear line of sight into how to answer that question without labeling yourself. You are the unquantifiable potential of the talents you possess. You are the charm and the lovableness of the traits you carry. You are the strength and the power of the skills you have earned. You are the passion and the purpose living within the values you hold. These limitless qualities of your individuality defy labeling. And through them, you can define who you truly are.

There is so much power in bringing all the pieces of you together. Doing so will open veins in you that you didn't even know you had. The more you embody your true self, the more you embrace your own light. The more light you embrace, the brighter you'll shine. And the brighter you shine, the brighter we all shine.

CHAPTER 11

Your Zone of Genius

Within your humanity lives your diversity. Within your diversity lives your individuality. And within your individuality lives your zone of genius. This is the nexus where your talents, traits, skills, and values unite into a singular, fully functional, laser-focused operating system. And it's a Michelin three-star recipe for every definition of success ever written. It's the very best of you coming together. How could it not?

Developing your zone of genius is not just about knowing the elements of your individuality but about knowing how to weave them together. Our talents, traits, skills, and values are currency in the world. With them, we can buy our way into certain social circles, relationships, jobs, and opportunities. And if we don't believe our currency—the individuality we are born with—holds value, we're most likely going to try and trade it in for one that does. It's human nature to relegate those parts of ourselves that don't fit into the current cultural construct to the background and take on other traits and values that seem like they will more readily bring us the friends, approval, and opportunities we seek. This does work—it gets us in those doors and social circles. But this strategy for success costs a premium price because you've hidden your gold and opted for plastic instead.

The plastic version of yourself is the one in which you forego your individuality in order to conform and fit a mold. Just like whipping out a credit card to buy something you can't afford, this will get you what you want. The instant gratification of belonging will be yours. But relying on plastic leaves you poorer in the long run. The value of your plastic self is determined by an outside source. Your street cred is reliant on whether or not you choose to operate in compliance with the rules of that outside source. The minute you don't, your credit can be revoked. Developing your zone of genius requires cutting up the plastic and, instead, mining your gold. Gold is rare. It's a finite resource that cannot be created. This is the very definition of you, and the talents, traits, skills, and values that comprise your human individuality. You are unrepeatable. Nothing could be more rare. And, just like gold, which isn't created but has to be discovered, the true genius in your individuality is waiting there, beneath the surface of your labels, ready to be mined. So, let's start digging.

Your zone of genius is comprised of three spheres: your who, your what, and your why. These three spheres are made up of a combination of your talents, traits, skills, and values. This is where all the aspects of your individuality—the best of your personal best—converge.

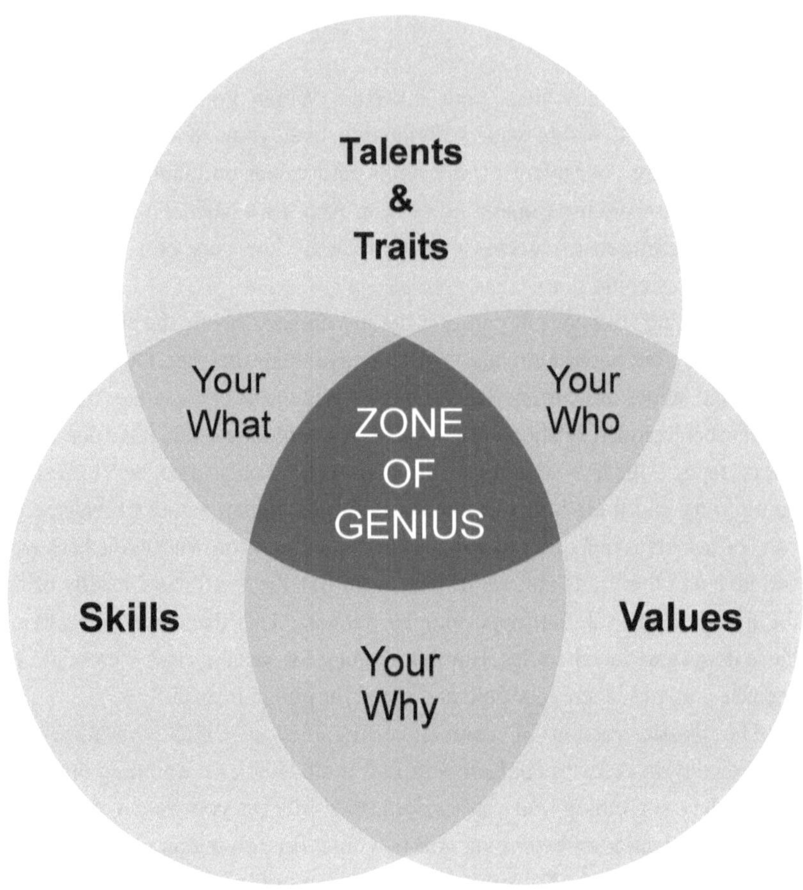

To help guide you to that convergence, we are going to treat the coming pages like a workshop in which you roll up your sleeves, pinpoint the elements of your individuality, map them to your who, what, and why, and then parlay that into a zone of genius.

ZONE OF GENIUS SPHERE 1: YOUR WHO

Your who consists of your talents and traits—all your signature abilities, proclivities, and goofy little quirks that are distinct to you. Up until now, we've talked about them in general terms. But here, the rubber is hitting the road. Now, you have to choose. What exactly are your unique talents? Talent, as a concept, is pretty straightforward, but traits have some nuances worth unpacking. You have mental traits that inform the unique lens through which you look at life and the resulting perspectives you build based on them. These are how you make sense of the world. You also have emotional traits that influence how you feel and process the people and events in your life. They play a large role in influencing the brain in personal decisions you make.

Combined, these create your personality. And your personality is how you put the being in "human being". Your personality determines the person you will be in any given situation. Your personality is how you experience life and how those in your life experience you. It makes you interesting, approachable, accessible, memorable, relatable, likable, barely tolerable, you name it.

It's not easy picking your most fundamental attributes out of thin air, so here's a list to help you. Pick no more than five key characteristics. While many may describe you, the goal is to hone in on the select few that define you. The core of the core. This list is to help prompt you, but don't let it limit you. If there is a mannerism or proclivity that isn't included in the list, write it in. This book would be six thousand pages long if I were to list every potential personality trait or quirk in existence.

DEFINING TRAITS

Active	Dramatic	Intelligent
Ambitious	Dynamic	Intuitive
Amusing	Determined	Kind
Adaptable	Dominating	Liberal
Adventurous	Dramatic	Logical
Appreciative	Emotional	Lovable
Artistic	Experimental	Loyal
Balanced	Earnest	Mature
Benevolent	Eloquent	Maternal
Calm	Empathetic	Mellow
Captivating	Energetic	Mystical
Caring	Enthusiastic	Mean
Challenging	Extroverted	Motivated
Charismatic	Forgiving	Observant
Charming	Funny	Open
Cheerful	Forthright	Optimistic
Clever	Friendly	Orderly
Compassionate	Fun-loving	Outgoing
Confident	Graceful	Private
Conscientious	Gentle	Proud
Considerate	Genuine	Passionate
Contemplative	Good-natured	Patient
Cooperative	Gregarious	Peaceful
Courageous	Helpful	Perceptive
Courteous	Heroic	Playful
Creative	Honest	Practical
Curious	Honorable	Protective
Competitive	Humble	Prudent
Conservative	Intense	Precocious
Daring	Irreverent	Pragmatic
Debonair	Idealistic	Quiet
Decisive	Imaginative	Rational
Deep	Independent	Realistic
Dignified	Insightful	Relaxed

<table>
<tr><td>Reliable</td><td>Sentimental</td><td>Tolerant</td></tr>
<tr><td>Resourceful</td><td>Serious</td><td>Trusting</td></tr>
<tr><td>Responsible</td><td>Sexy</td><td>Tough</td></tr>
<tr><td>Romantic</td><td>Shrewd</td><td>Understanding</td></tr>
<tr><td>Reserved</td><td>Simple</td><td>Vivacious</td></tr>
<tr><td>Resilient</td><td>Spontaneous</td><td>Warm</td></tr>
<tr><td>Shy</td><td>Sociable</td><td>Wise</td></tr>
<tr><td>Sensual</td><td>Stoic</td><td>Witty</td></tr>
<tr><td>Skeptical</td><td>Strong</td><td>Whimsical</td></tr>
<tr><td>Stubborn</td><td>Sweet</td><td>Youthful</td></tr>
<tr><td>Selfless</td><td>Sympathetic</td><td></td></tr>
<tr><td>Sensitive</td><td>Thoughtful</td><td></td></tr>
</table>

Now that you have your five key traits identified, let's focus on your talents. Again, you are going to have to be judicious and choose no more than five. As discussed, they will fall into two categories: obvious talents and hidden talents. The abilities that are obvious will be easy to identify. The hidden ones not so much because, as the word implies, for whatever reason, you can't see them. But just because they're in your blind spot doesn't mean they are hidden from everyone's sight.

There are ways to tap into this outside perspective. One is to think about the things you get complimented on that give you imposter syndrome. This is a classic tell that points to a personal strength that you aren't owning. If you are feeling like a fraud for abilities people see as legit, then you're missing something.

Your zone of genius requires you to own all of yourself, not just the parts you are comfortable with. If you find you are having a hard time owning all of who you are, well, welcome to the human condition. We all have demons to slay. So, chances are you will most likely have to dismantle these feelings of inferiority and silence the voices of doubt that are bound to come up as you learn to own your unique brand of kickasserie.

Again, I've included a list of talents to help prompt you. Again, please don't let it limit you. If you are naturally good at something that isn't on the list, write it in. Remember, no talent is too small. Nothing is insignificant when it comes to your personal strengths.

INNATE TALENTS

Artistic	Composing	Planning
Acting	Detail-oriented	Pottery
Adaptability	Dancing	Organization
Analyzing	Diplomacy	Relaxation
Athleticism	Decorating	Problem solving
Articulation	Designing	Persuasiveness
Arguing	Dexterity	Planning
Agility	Drawing	Performing
Building	Entertaining	Public speaking
Carpentry	Eye for fashion	Rhyming
Comedy	Gardening	Rhythm
Conceptual	Good judgment	Repairing things
Conversational	Healing	Singing
Comedy	Inventiveness	Storytelling
Communication	Imagination	Strategic thinking
Cooking	Intuition	Social intelligence
Coping	Innovation	Spatial intelligence
Crafting	Impersonations	Sculpting
Creativity	Leading	Technically minded
Composition	Mathematics	Visualization
Connecting to others	Memory	Writing
Critical thinking	Metal work	Woodworking
Creating space	Mechanics	
Coordination	Musical abilities	

You've now honed in on the talents you know you have. It's time to make sure you haven't inadvertently left any hidden ones behind. This will require enlisting a friend. Pick that one person in your life who always plays it straight and tells you the truth no matter what. Without sharing your picks, share the list of traits provided and ask that person to choose the talents they see in you. Remind them to write anything that might not be on the list. Once done, compare lists. If there is anything on your trusted partner's list that wasn't on yours, dig deeper. Ask your friend to share examples of incidents where they saw that talent in action in your life. It helps to have context when you're trying to uncover your blind spots.

Now comes the need for deep discernment, because it's time to reconcile how you see yourself with who you really are. In the end, and always, it's you who decides what is true for yourself and your life. So, if there are talents on someone else's list you truly don't embody or consider at the center of your core strengths, adhere to your own wisdom and don't add it to your list. But if you discover things that carry even an inkling of truth, you have reached a juncture in which you realize you might not know yourself as well as you thought you did. And this is awesome. Chances are you are about to gain access to a superpower you didn't know you had.

Take some time to explore those surprise talents. If it feels like they might fit, try them on for a while. Sift through your memory and see where you may have been leaning into this talent without even knowing it. There are two signs that help reveal if you've hit on something: One is feeling incredulous and excited. The other, on the opposite end of the spectrum, is feeling anxious or overly adamant that this can't possibly be true. The excitement is a sign that you've uncovered a hidden talent and are ready to own it. The upset is a sign that you've uncovered a hidden talent but would rather keep denying it exists. If there were no truth for you in what your buddy's list revealed, you wouldn't have a strong reaction either way. It would be more like a lukewarm "That's interesting," kind of thing. But if strong emotions on either end of the spectrum come up, then your body is responding to a nugget of truth.

The negative responses are a sign that you have some sort of fear or inferiority residing within you that's holding you back from accepting an aspect of your greatness. No big deal; put on your big person pants and look it straight in the eye. Remember, feelings are just energy. And energy can transmute into anything you want it to be.

So, do the work to curate a list of talents that genuinely define you to your core and have been with you from the get-go. Between known and hidden traits, you still want to keep the list to five or under. We all possess many traits to one degree or another, but the ones you want to identify with are those that define you to your core. Once you have them in hand, it'll be time to move on to the second sphere in your zone of genius.

ZONE OF GENIUS SPHERE 2: YOUR WHAT

Your what is comprised of your skills. As opposed to the abilities you are born with (your talents), these are abilities you learn. Skills are acquired through conscious choice. They're picked up along the course of living through experience, apprenticeships, education, mentoring, and personal and professional development. The avenues for developing skills are unlimited because there's nothing you can't learn if you set your mind to it.

This is why it can be daunting to try and figure out what to do with your life. When you look at all the possible paths, it can be so overwhelming, you shut down. You need an inner compass to guide you and help narrow the options. That compass is the list of traits and talents you identified in the first sphere of your zone of genius. When you set out to determine the educational or developmental path you want to take in life, instead of asking, "What do I want to do?" ask yourself, "Who am I?" Let the person you are and the things you are good at guide your way. Within a zone of genius, your skills enable you to put your talents to use. It's also a powerful way to bring positive energy into the world.

We talk a lot these days about sending light. When someone is going through a hard time, we say things like, "Sending you love and light." It's a wonderful sentiment, but often it's said without any understanding of its mechanics. At your deepest and purest level, you are light. So, when you send light to another, what you are actually doing is sending the very best of yourself out into the world in hopes of making a difference, which, coincidentally, is exactly what happens when you develop skills that allow you to express your talents. Your innate talents and traits are the best of who you are. Sending them out into the world with positive intention to help make things better is literally a way to let your light flow.

Beyond the metaphysical, there are some solid practical reasons for building skill sets around your innate talents. For example, when you source your development from the bedrock of who you are, it eradicates going into college without any idea of what you want to study. You can maximize that Herculean investment from day one. It also gives you the decision power to discern if college is even the right path for you. Because the fact is, some skill sets might not require the aforementioned Herculean investment.

Not every career path needs formalized education. There are plenty of successful people that have proven that: Oprah Winfrey, Steve Jobs, Henry Ford, John D. Rockefeller, Tiger Woods, Bill Gates, Jay-Z, Beyoncé, Ellen DeGeneres, Ralph Lauren, Frank Loyd Wright, Magic Johnson, Steven Spielberg. None of them finished college. But they have more in common than just that fact. All were loyal to their own talent, passion, or vision. Rather than following the traditional path society pressures us into, they bet on themselves and pursued the thing that would let them bring their talent, passion, or vision to life.

It's not a popular thing to say, but the truth is, college can be a waste of money if it isn't going to help you develop your personal talents and passion. If the innate abilities you have are better developed through a trade school or an apprenticeship or a startup, then that's the road to follow. There are so many ways to bring your diverse talent to life. For example, being good at music doesn't mean you have to be a musician. You could be a music teacher, a song writer, a record label executive, a band manager, an instrument maker, a sound technician, a music store owner, a talent agent, or a live venue manager, just to name a few.

Some of these paths might call for more formalized education, but many of them don't. If you find that your authentic path takes you off culture's beaten path, that's A-OK. Getting a degree just to have one is conformity at its most expensive.

Whether you are still trying to figure out what you want to do with your life, are already knee-deep in a career and want to further develop yourself within it, or looking to shift into a second career, step one is the same. Look to yourself for the answer. More specifically, look to the talents and traits that you were born with. Rid yourself of all the cultural chatter that has worked its way into your psyche and tried to tell you what you should and shouldn't do with your life. Deliberately choose to develop skills that tap into your natural abilities.

Even if you haven't yet figured out exactly what you want to do, you can start to develop your natural abilities. While you take the necessary time to pick a path, focus on developing fundamental skills that connect to your talents. For example, let's say you were born with the natural ability to draw. You've always been really good at it and you love it, but you don't yet know how you want to parlay that into a professional career. That one talent could open dozens of doors: you could become an architect, an animator, a costume designer, a sketch artist, an art teacher, a cartoonist, an art director, or a fashion designer. Each will require you to specialize in an area eventually, but until you are ready to narrow your focus onto a specific profession, there are foundational skills you can start to build that will strengthen your talent and may even help you decide which path to choose. You can begin learning how to draw proportions, develop perspective, understand color theory, or master creative software. All of these fundamental skills will serve you well regardless of the path you eventually choose. More importantly, by investing in your talents, you stay true to the path you were born to walk.

This is the beginning of betting on yourself and trusting that the seemingly random gifts you were born with are actually anything but random. Your innate abilities are, in fact, hints from the Universe—little clues nudging you toward a career and a life that holds personal meaning and a sense of purpose.

As you focus on what to develop, think plural rather than singular. The idea is to curate a set of skills that will give you the flexibility to apply them in a number of different ways. One skill will only allow you to walk a small number of paths, but a robust skill set will empower you to pursue a great number of industries and careers.

Eventually, you will have to sharpen your focus and make a choice as to what you want to do with your life in order to further develop specific skills. But before you can do that, you'll need to figure out what your motivation is to build that skill set and put it into action day after day, which leads us to sphere 3.

ZONE OF GENIUS SPHERE 3: YOUR WHY

Life can be hard, even when you spend it doing what you love. There will be challenges, losses, and unforeseen circumstances that bring you to your knees. There will also be the plain old garden variety exhaustion that stems from building relationships, raising kids, caring for pets, maintaining homes, and all the other time- and energy-consuming privileges that come with having people to love and care for. Even when you wouldn't trade your life for anything, there will be days when getting out of bed to face it all is the last thing you want to do. And this is why you need a deeper motivating force that sustains you and drives you to bring everything you've got into each day regardless of what that day brings. You will pour much of your life's energy into your career, so you want to be sure that it returns the favor and energizes you in return. And this is why, before committing to what you want to do with your life, you need to consider why you want to do it. And in a zone of genius, that answer is never to make money.

Financial well-being, as important as it is, is a byproduct of your career, not the motivator for it. What you do with your life professionally has to matter to you personally, which is where your values come in. Your why comes from your values, the deep and driving convictions that you hold most true in your heart. There are things that matter to you—ways in which you want to leave your mark and make the world just a little better than where you found it. By getting crystal clear on what they are and why they matter so much to you, you can make a deliberate choice as to where and how you want to put your talents and skills to use. Developing your why gives you a sense of purpose. And your purpose will then become your North Star.

Your why will let you know which industries and companies are right for you. Through your values, purpose will guide you as to whether you want to start or work for a company, and if the latter, they'll point you toward which companies are the right fit for you. This will determine the type of employee, teammate, partner, and leader you will be and guide who you hire and choose as a mentor. Your why becomes the GPS through which you live your life. It will help you take the loose idea of what you want to do with your talents and skills and bring your unique path into focus.

Just like choosing traits and talents, it can be a challenge to whittle down your list of values to a select few. For the most part, values are positive things. Optimism. Justice. Kindness. Truthfulness. Generosity. Hope. Compassion. Fairness. Who doesn't want to stand for these things? They're just a drop in the ocean of good and positive values that you can choose from when picking the ones that most truly represent the truth in your being. However, as hard as it may be, just like with your who and your what, when it comes to your why, you have to make hard choices. Having too many values does you no good. When you try to stand for everything, you end up standing for nothing. When narrowing down your core values, just remember that choosing a few doesn't mean rejecting others. The point is to get very clear on the four or five you want to orbit around.

CORE VALUES

Acceptance	Friendship	Peace
Accountability	Forgiveness	Serenity
Authenticity	Fun	Sincerity
Adventure	Generosity	Selflessness
Autonomy	Gratitude	Self-awareness
Balance	Graciousness	Self-love
Beauty	Growth	Stewardship
Bravery	Happiness	Trust
Brotherhood	Hope	Leadership
Caring	Honor	Reliability
Charity	Harmony	Respect
Collaboration	Honesty	Responsibility
Connection	Humility	Security
Compassion	Integrity	Stability
Cooperation	Independence	Togetherness
Courage	Joy	Tradition
Duty	Justice	Truth
Empowerment	Kindness	Trust
Equality	Knowledge	Tolerance
Faith	Loyalty	Unity
Family	Love	Vulnerability
Fairness	Openness	
Freedom	Protection	

Before you move forward, make sure you've picked no more than five values. It's important to be discerning and to make sure you are focused on the ones that truly define you from the inside out. If you're having a hard time choosing them, chances are you are still unknowingly holding on to some outside-in values. By that I mean those values that you were born into through things such as nationality and creed. Here's a hack to help ensure that your values truly define the diverse and individual person that you are: Look to see which of your values feel more general than others. For example, love. This is a true and wonderful value, but it is also one that takes many different forms, which makes it a bit more general. Ask yourself how you, specifically, show love? If it's through giving, then generosity is probably more of a core value to you. If you love through caretaking, then protection or stewardship might be closer to your core. If you love through honoring all life, then respect or acceptance are more likely to speak to your unique value set.

Once you have your value list tight, it's blending time. With all three spheres of your zone of genius clearly defined, we turn to combining them in a way that empowers you to build worldly success through the unique spirit you are.

CHAPTER 12

Monetizing Your Originality

You were born to succeed. Literally. Every human being is pre-wired with unique interests, passions, traits, and abilities to turn their given lifetime into a win. By winning, I don't mean countless riches and fame. It's a huge win in life to love what you do and to be fairly paid and have enough to take care of yourself and your family doing it. Unfortunately, that is not currently the case. A vast majority of people dislike and are totally disengaged from their chosen jobs and careers. And what are they getting for all that unhappiness? Not much. Worldwide, millions of hardworking people are giving their all and still aren't able to pay for medicine, buy healthy food, and keep roofs over their heads. The current system of success is setting so many of us up to fail. Which means it's time to redefine what success means.

As it stands, culture has defined success by money, power, and status. And with that definition firmly rooted, culture then created the systems that control each of these three things. Which means the bias is boss. The patterns of privilege and crony capitalism built into our culture have rigged the game so that most of us have no chance to meet the established definition of success. We live in a world where the richest 1 percent of our population own twice as much as the bottom 90 percent. And the landslide of inequity is just getting worse. Recent studies show that worldwide, this same 1 percent has accumulated close to two-thirds of all new wealth created. Let's break that down: For every dollar hardworking people in the bottom 90 percent make, a billionaire makes around $1.7 million. That. Is. Bonkers.

There is no way that those in the top echelon of success all work harder than the rest of us. There is no way that they, across the board, are smarter than the rest of us. There is no way that they are more talented than the rest of us. For the most part, they just somehow have access to circumstances, connections, or the luck to game the system as it currently works. In other words, they got dealt a good hand at the card table of Life.

But here's the thing: Life is not meant to be a game of chance that opens its coffers for a few lucky winners. Life, as it was meant to be lived, is designed for us all to succeed. It's the man-made systems we live within that play favorites. The growing degrees of wealth inequity in our world have made it crystal clear that those systems need to be dismantled. When the vast majority of intelligent, talented, hardworking humans have little to no chance of winning the game, our only option is to stop playing and find a new game.

The elite schools only have so many seats. The elite companies only have so many openings. If we want society's definition of success, we have to pit ourselves against one another and fight tooth and nail to become one of the elite. These cultural systems that are rooted in ruthless competition only serve to further deepen our divide. They have us chasing a definition of success that requires us to best one another rather than focusing on our own personal best.

Society's definition of success favors the few. But Life's definition of success is different. It's designed for all of us. It does not rely on labels but in fact relies on the absence of them. Life's definition of success is to live your truth, know who you are, trust who you are, and build a life that brings you happiness and financial security by expressing who you are. Within this definition, there are as many different paths to success as there are people in the world. And yours will unfold when you take the spheres of your zone of genius and weave them together to create a singular focus that points you toward your unique path.

ZONING IN ON YOUR ZONE OF GENIUS

Monetizing your originality means finding a way to be valued professionally for who you are personally. It leads to building a career in which your traits are welcomed as an asset, your skills are put to use, and through your values, you can find meaning in your day-to-day endeavors. This lays the foundation for a new, more inclusive societal definition of success, one in which your sense of purpose and your paycheck support you in living a happy life.

Exactly how do you monetize your originality so that you can define success on your terms? By taking the three spheres of your zone of genius as you defined them and combining them into one singular focus. Doing so will point you toward industries and careers in which your unique abilities can be put to work in ways that hold meaning for you. This meets the first criteria for a new definition of success—loving what you do for a living. And, because your zone of genius is the aggregate of the best you have to offer, you'll be bringing your greatest strengths to that job. This positions you to excel, which sets you up for the second part of a new definition of success: being fairly compensated for your contributions.

The first step is to stop looking at your who, what, and why as three separate, disconnected spheres. They are designed to work together. When baking a cake, the butter, sugar, and flour may start out in separate bowls, but the magic happens when you blend them together in just the right way. The same is true here. When you stop compartmentalizing these parts of yourself and instead, start connecting them, paths and possibilities that you hadn't seen before appear.

Your traits and talents will point you toward the jobs and trades you are best suited for. And with that in place, your values will point you toward the companies and organizations that will bring purpose to the job or trade you choose. In other words, your traits and talents will point you toward a specific line of work. And your values will point you toward an industry in which that line of work will feel personally meaningful.

Let's walk through an example to show you how it works. The first thing we do is assess the list of traits and skills you identified and come up with a list of different careers that need the combination of things you have to offer. As an example, let's say that in developing your first sphere, you've chosen the following:

» **Traits:** curious, helpful, extroverted, tenacious, hopeless romantic

» **Talents:** decorating, writing, networking, multitasking, detail oriented

On the surface there seems to be no rhyme or reason to how these disparate things might work together. Again, think baking. It's all in how you blend them together. Being helpful and extroverted, combined with the ability to decorate spaces and connect people, could make you an amazing real estate agent. Being detail-oriented and a hopeless romantic would make for a great wedding planner. Being curious, tenacious, and able to write makes for great investigative reporting. These three vastly different career paths have one incredibly important thing in common: they each stem from the same elements of a single zone of genius.

So, if this were your zone of genius, knowing you can do any of these things and still honor and excel as the person you are, how do you choose? This is where your why comes in. Let's bring that sphere into the picture:

» **Traits:** curious, helpful, extroverted, tenacious, hopeless romantic

» **Talents:** decorating, writing, networking, multitasking, detail oriented

» **Values:** truth, justice, courage

These values would point you more toward investigative journalism. Exposing the truth requires courage, so you would be living two values at once. And bringing manipulated spin or the shrouded behavior of companies, leaders, and systems into the light of day so they can be fairly tried in the court of public opinion is bringing about a more just world.

But let's say you had the same traits, talents, and skills but a whole different set of values:

» **Traits:** curious, helpful, extroverted, tenacious, hopeless romantic

» **Talents:** decorating, writing, networking, multitasking, detail oriented

» **Values:** kindness, independence, stability

These values might point you more toward a career as a real estate agent. Because you value independence, this path would allow you to create a schedule that doesn't tie you to an office or a desk. It allows you to use your extroverted nature to help others find stability in times of change.

Let's look one more time at how a third set of values applied to the same traits and talents would guide you down yet another path:

» **Traits:** curious, helpful, extroverted, tenacious, hopeless romantic
» **Talents:** decorating, writing, networking, multitasking, detail oriented
» **Values:** love, joy, collaboration

With the core values of love, joy, and collaboration driving you, becoming a wedding planner would more likely be the purpose-driven path. You would spend all your energy, every day, supporting couples who love one another. Your entire mission would be to help them create what could be one of the most joyful days of their lives. Every day would be spent collaborating with couples, venues, bakers, bands, decorators, and other vendors that will need to come together to make the couple's dream wedding.

Your why is the linchpin to your recipe for success. Out of all the many, many career paths your talents, traits, and abilities could lead you down, it will shine a light on the one or two that will be genuinely purpose-driven for you. And if you can find that sweet spot, you will be doing more than making money—you will be living richly. When there is a sense that what you are doing with your life truly matters to you, meeting the day-to-day demands of that life will feed your spirit even as it depletes your energy levels. That's the magic that happens when you custom build a life that's right for you.

Another trick to choosing a career path that holds meaning is flip the script and, instead of looking at what you think the world needs more of, focus on what you think it needs less of. Often, the thing that matters to us the most is hidden within the thing that most irks us. If bigotry is something that makes you hot under the collar, then find a way to use your abilities to help eradicate the systems that allow for that behavior. Be it as a lawyer, politician, or human resources leader, you should unleash your zone of genius down a path that empowers you to help marginalized people get fair shots and equal opportunities. If it absolutely breaks your heart to think of animals or children being abused, it would make sense to point your zone of genius toward animal rescue, veterinary medicine, social work, or some other path that allows you to help kids or animals. I call this turning your nemesis into your muse. Let the behavior or condition in the world that really ticks you off or breaks your heart inspire you toward a career that helps bring it to an end once and for all.

When you focus your zone of genius on the cultural demon that most incenses you, you position yourself to do your part to lessen that evil. We all need to do our part, regardless of how small or insignificant it may seem in the grand scheme of things. There is honor and nobility in doing your part, no matter how small. That alone is enough. It may be our job collectively to save the world, but it is not your job as an individual. Bettering our world is a team sport. Everybody has to do their part and play their position. With the underlying understanding that we are all in this together, the accumulated effect of the little things we do now is how we eventually win the game.

Once you've pinpointed a purpose-driven path that can bring both financial security and personal fulfillment, it's time to revisit your skill set. You may need to do a little tweaking now that you have a clearer sense of where you want to take your life. From this new vantage point, you will be empowered to see if it makes more sense for you to pursue a degree, attend trade school, be an apprentice, an acting coach, an investor to fund a startup, etc. Think it through. What hard and soft skills do you need in your toolbox to set you up for success on your chosen path? What is the most practical way for you to develop them? Who in your circle of friends and family can help? Map it out step-by-step. Take each step one at a time, knowing that every stride you make is another vote of confidence in yourself as the truly valuable, diverse individual you are. Disregard all the voices and cultural noise that doubts your ability to build a successful life based on your gifts. No matter how overlooked or unpolished they may be, the innate skills, personality traits, and natural aptitudes you possess are the biggest clues life can give you for developing a fulfilling, passion-driven existence.

Life is not stupid. In fact, it is wise beyond measure. So, you can trust that Life did not endow you with talents and traits that are useless or frivolous. However humble your unique attributes may seem, they're your gifts. If you let them, they will point you to a life that holds both personal meaning and professional success.

Your who, what, and why in your zone of genius unite every part of you. This isn't just good for you, it's good for everyone. Because unified people unify people. Once you become at peace with yourself, it's easier to be at peace with others. When you're happy in your own skin and feel at home on this planet of ours, you will have less of an urge to judge others and more willingness to give people the grace and leeway to be who they came here to be. When you embrace your own humanity, you open the door and embrace all humanity.

A Label-Free Farewell

My parting and forever wish is that you find your way free of the labels that obscure your view of all you truly are as a human and all we truly are as a race. The time for opening our collective eyes is now. Life is calling for us to see our shared and unifying truth. We are more than just our genders. We are more than our monetary worth. We are more than our working class. We are more than our skin color. We are more than our religious affiliations. We are more than our nationalities. We are more than any diploma we earned. We are more than any spectrum or disability. Though these labels can be central to how we identify ourselves, they cannot contain us. We are more than all of them put together.

We are more than human. We are beings. Infinite, eternal, life-spanning, always-evolving, ever-expanding energetic superstars that occasionally don a body in order to experience life and all the good and bad it has to offer. We are beings sharing an existence on this planet. This is our collective truth. This is our unifying force.

Our defining light grows as a result of the humans we are being. We are the wisdom we have amassed through the years we have logged. We are the love we have cultivated through the relationships we've built. We are the joy we have accrued through the laughter we've shared. We are the strengths we have garnered through the challenges we've overcome. We are the doubts we harbor from the failures we cling to. We are the hurt we hold from the losses we've incurred. We are a conglomeration of all we have been. Human is our label. But being is our truth.

We have so much more in common than the world would have us believe. We all have dreams. We all have hopes. We all have plans. We all have pasts. We've all been better and worse versions of ourselves. We've all known sickness and health. We all want to feel safe and loved. We all know what it is to laugh and cry, to win and lose, to have and to have not. We all want to scale that mountain in front of us and shout to the sky that we did it.

At the heart of our commonality is the Universal truth that we are all unique individuals. You are born with the inalienable and divine right to rule your kingdom of one. Banish the labels that have invaded your space and learn to be who you really are. When you embrace your originality, it becomes harder to judge others for expressing theirs. In this, you've cultivated acceptance for others. When you step out of systematic labels, it becomes harder to be manipulated. In this, you've cultivated autonomy. When you source your professional path from your personal truth, you find self-worth. In this, you've cultivated an understanding of human value. Acceptance. Autonomy. Understanding human value. These things will bring us together if we let them. Let's choose to be stronger. Let's choose to be closer. Let's choose to step out of the labels that divide us and into the humanity that unites us. A better world awaits.

ABOUT THE AUTHOR

Merry Carole Powers is a creative and strategic thought leader with more than two decades of experience working with some of the furthest-reaching global brands and multinational advertising networks in our world, including Deloitte, Beam Suntory, McDonald's, and multiple advertising agencies across Publicis Groupe and Omnicom Group. Her passion lies in positioning companies and the people within them to achieve greater degrees of success while also making a purposeful, positive impact on the world we share. She is a believer in the power of creativity, a champion of originality, and a head-over-heels lover of dogs, particularly Boston Terriers. When not hammering away at a keyboard, she's most likely pummeling a punching bag, exploring a new vintage of whiskey, or yammering away with her fiancé under the trees of their Pennsylvania home. Her previous book, *The Branding Sutra: The Principles of Branding for the Business of Life*, can be found on Amazon. You can learn more about this title at WeVillePress.com.